"Sabra Ricci's passion for cooking f   ....ars and her lifelong
fascination with astrology come together in her truly extraordinary book."
—Jenny McCarthy

"Sabra is a truly talented chef and an amazing and inspiring person. So
glad our planets crossed!"   —Orlando Bloom

"Sabra, thank you for spoiling us. Every bite was a new experience."
—Julia Roberts and her husband, Danny Moder

"Sabra is an alchemist. She cares deeply about everything she creates and
lives in service to all of us—breakfast, lunch, and dinner."

—Jim Carrey

"Sabra knows how to take cooking and entertaining to the level of a
party! Her recipes are soulful and easy to make on your own. I've never
had as much fun in the kitchen as I had with Sabra!"

—Robert Bates,
James Beard Award-winner and
director of *Ingredients*

"We have been proud to feature Sabra Ricci on Tarot.com, because not
only is she a world-class chef, she is also a superb astrologer!"

—Paul O'Brien,
founder of Tarot.com and
executive director of *Divination.com*

"After being lucky enough to meet Sabra and have her cook for me in
Hawaii, I was extra lucky to have the most accurate reading done. She was
precise to the month of when things were going to happen. I'm a be-
liever."   —Cher Coulter,
winner of the 2010 Stylist of the Year award
at the annual Hollywood Style Awards and
cofounder and stylist at *Jewelmint.com*

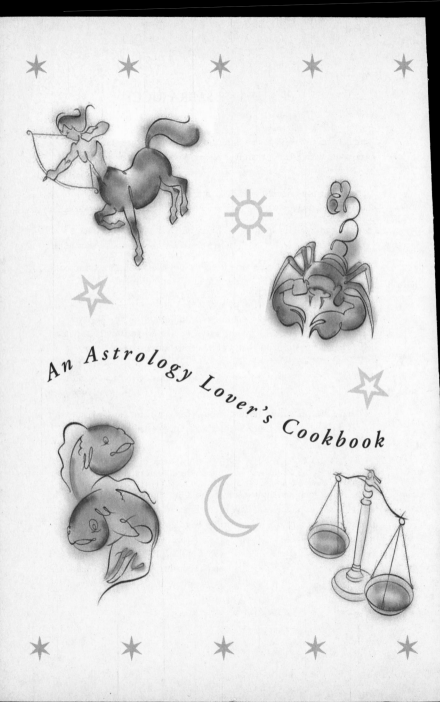

An Astrology Lover's Cookbook

Lobster
for Leos,
Cookies for
Capricorns

Sabra Ricci

THOMAS DUNNE BOOKS ST. MARTIN'S GRIFFIN   NEW YORK

THOMAS DUNNE BOOKS.
An imprint of St. Martin's Press.

LOBSTER FOR LEOS, COOKIES FOR CAPRICORNS. Copyright © 2011
by Sabra Ricci. All rights reserved. Printed in the United States of
America. For information, address St. Martin's Press, 175 Fifth
Avenue, New York, N.Y. 10010.

www.thomasdunnebooks.com
www.stmartins.com

Illustrations by Elizabeth Ricci Souza and Jennifer Ricci

Design by Ellen Cipriano

LIBRARY OF CONGRESS CATALOGING-IN-PUBLICATION DATA

Ricci, Sabra.
    Lobster for Leos, cookies for Capricorns : an astrology lover's
cookbook / Sabra Ricci. — 1st ed.
        p. cm.
    Includes index.
    ISBN 978-1-250-00213-6
    1. Cooking.   2. Astrology.   I. Title.
    TX652.5.R53 2012
    641.5—dc23

                                                2011032783

First Edition: January 2012

10 9 8 7 6 5 4 3 2 1

For Alexandra Marie

★

Contents

Acknowledgments   xv

Foreword   xvii

Introduction   xxi

Astrological Guidelines and Definitions   xxv

1 ✳ ARIES   1

Acai Berry Smoothie   8

Double Chocolate Cocoa
    Nib Cookies   9

Kona Coffee–Rubbed Flank Steaks with
    Cilantro-Lime Vinaigrette   10

Artichoke Heart Hummus   12

Matcha Crème Brûlée   13

Panko Rosemary Crusted Rack of Lamb   14

Wild Salmon on Cedar Planks with
    Corn and Avocado Salsa   16
Honey Walnut Shrimp   18

2 ✶ TAURUS   20
Arame Napa Cabbage Slaw with
    Ginger-Sesame Vinaigrette   27
Zucchini Bread with Toasted Brazil Nuts   28
Celtic Sea Salt Butterscotch Pot de Crème   30
Coconut-Crusted Onaga (Hawaiian Ruby
    Snapper) with Guava Sauce   31
Wild Mushroom Risotto   33
Spicy Shrimp with Hearts of Romaine and
    Creamy Avocado Dressing   35
Warm Swiss Chard and Portobello Salad
    with Pancetta   38
Butternut Squash and Wild Rice Pilaf   40

3 ✶ GEMINI   42
Marinated Roasted Brussels Sprouts   48
Cannellini Bean Ragout with Grilled
    Rosemary Shrimp   50
Grilled Mahi Mahi with Orange and
    Ginger Beurre Blanc   52

Cantaloupe, Tomato, and Basil Salad with
    Feta Cheese   54

Cornmeal Pancakes with Blueberries and
    Sour Cream   55

Cucumber-Tomato Salad with Fresh
    Oregano   56

Panna Cotta with Raspberry Purée   58

Thyme and Panko Crusted Chicken
    Milanese   60

4 ✶ CANCER   62

Chilled Soba Noodle Salad with Tofu and
    Sesame Vinaigrette   69

Green Tea, Pineapple, and Ginger Martini
    for Two   70

Shaved Fennel, Blood Orange, and Baby
    Arugula Salad   71

Leek, Potato, Wild Mushroom, and Fontina
    Frittata   72

Grilled Teriyaki Chicken with
    Pineapple-Mango Salsa   74

Radish, Tomato, and Butterleaf Salad with
    Bay Shrimp and Maytag Blue Cheese   76

Watercress with Beet Carpaccio and Sherry
    Vinaigrette   77

Watermelon with Shaved Maui Onion and
   Lime   79

5 ✴ LEO   80
Ahi Tartare on Wonton with Wasabi Crème
   Fraîche and Tobiko   87
Almond Pound Cake with Caramelized
   Pears and Mascarpone   89
Creamy Polenta with Black Bean Ragout   92
Lobster Macaroni and Cheese   94
Crab-Stuffed Opakapaka with Lobster
   Bordelaise   96
Seared Scallops with Saffron Butter   98
Papaya Stuffed with Shrimp Ceviche   100
Heirloom Tomato and Bufala di Mozzarella
   Napoleon   101

6 ✴ VIRGO   103
Braised Baby Bok Choy with Red Peppers
   and Oyster Mushrooms   110
Orecchiette Pasta with Broccolini and
   Pecorino   112
Grilled New York Strips with Portobello
   Mushrooms and Horseradish Sauce   113

French Green Lentils and Roasted
    Vegetable Stew   115
Frosted Lavender and Lemon Zest
    Shortbread Cookies   116
Pumpkin Spice Cupcakes with Cream
    Cheese Frosting and Crystallized
    Ginger   118
Split Pea Soup with Roasted Pork Belly   120
Lemon Thyme–Roasted Turkey Breast with
    Butternut Squash   121

7 ✳ LIBRA   124
Warm Burrata over Roasted Tomatoes and
    Basil with Olive Oil and Balsamic
    Syrup   130
Roasted Cauliflower and Maui Onion
    Gratin with Smoked Gouda   132
Grilled Cherry and Arugula Salad with
    Cambozola Cheese   133
Cranberry-Pistachio Scones   135
Roasted Garlic Mashed Potatoes with
    Caramelized Onions and Bacon   136
Creamy Five Onion Soup   138
Creamy Roasted Red Pepper Sauce with
    Italian Sausage over Fusilli   140

Coconut- and Macadamia Nut–Crusted
  Shrimp with Lilikoi Cocktail
  Sauce   142

8 ✳ SCORPIO   144
Grilled Asparagus with Black Truffle Oil   151
Caviar Party for Two   152
Chocolate-Rum Pot de Crème   154
Pancetta-Wrapped Figs with Gorgonzola   156
Triple Ginger Chocolate Shortbread
  Cookies   157
Asian Honey Chicken Kabobs   158
Malpeque Oysters on the Half Shell with
  Ginger Mignonette Sauce   159
Strawberry Rose Petal Cupcakes with Rose
  Butter Cream Frosting   161

9 ✳ SAGITTARIUS   164
Apple Crisp à la Mode   171
Lobster Guacamole   172
Warm Baby Beet Salad over Grilled
  Portobellos with Brie   174
Cinnamon Sauce   175
Chocolate-Dipped Coconut Biscotti   176

Pesto-Crusted Halibut with Tomato,
  Olive, and Caper Relish 178
Meyer Lemon Orzo Risotto 180
Pasta Arrabbiata with Shrimp, Rocket,
  and Grana Padano 181

10 ✳ CAPRICORN 183
Madelyn's Banana Bread 190
Chicken and Napa Cabbage Egg Rolls
  with Ginger-Chili Vinaigrette 192
Roasted Pork Tenderloin with Glazed
  Apples and Cloves 194
Molasses Cookies 196
Pumpkin-Bran Muffins with Pepito Seeds 198
Spinach and Feta Frittata 200
Garlicky Tofu Stir-Fry 202
Bhutanese Rice (Red Rice) 203

11 ✳ AQUARIUS 204
Miso-Marinated Pan-Seared Sea Bass 211
Blueberry Muffins with Lemon Curd 212
Creamy Coconut-Carrot Soup 214
Spicy (Cayenne) Cocktail Nut Mix 215
Chicken Katsu 216

Smoked Molokai Sweet Potatoes   218
Chopped Hearts of Palm with Blue
    Cheese Dressing and Bacon   219
Pistachio Mousse Tarts   220

12 ✳ PISCES   222
Zesty Chile-Cheese Cornbread   229
Crab Cakes with Julienned Mango
    and Red Pepper Aioli   230
Herb-Crusted Leg of Lamb   232
Roasted Potatoes and Cipollini Onions
    with Cumin   234
Tzatziki Sauce   235
Chipotle–White Bean Grilled Chicken
    Chili   236
Buttermilk Cupcakes with Maple Butter
    Cream and Bacon   238
Oatmeal–Dried Cherry Cookies with
    White Chocolate Chips   240

Resources   243
Index   247

Acknowledgments

This book has been a labor of love, combining two lifelong passions, astrology and food. I would first and foremost like to thank my mother, Elizabeth, for her unwavering support, encouragement, and round-the-clock feedback and contributions. My husband, Ferenc, for his love, patience, and continued confidence. My daughter, Ally, for cheering me on, being my guinea pig, and being the best child a mother could wish for. To Shannon, my sister, my friend, and my confidante; your enthusiasm, optimism, and words of encouragement bring never-ending light to my life. My grandpa George, for introducing me to the magic of food and teaching me at a young age that if you can feed people, you will always be loved. I miss you, Grandpa! To my loving Italian family, for imparting your culinary passion, handing down the family recipes, and most of all, for the good times in the kitchen and memories I will cherish forever. I love you all!

Special thanks to my literary agent, Susan Crawford, and to my editor, Marcia Markland, at Thomas Dunne Books, for believing in me and this project, and giving me the chance to share what I love. To everyone at Thomas Dunne Books and St. Martin's Press for helping bring this book to fruition. My most sincere gratitude to Jenny McCarthy, for your great advice, support, and being such an inspiration. Thank you to Elizabeth Ricci Souza and Jennifer Ricci for coming in at the eleventh hour with your unique and creative designs.

Thanks to Irene Aroner and everyone at Tropical Villa Vacations. Your continual support has brought me where I am today. To Robin Layton, the most gifted photographer I know. To Terri Trespicio, for your unbelievable openness, meticulous eye for detail, and helping shape this book in its infancy. You're a gem! To my astrologer and lifelong friend James (Dharman) Reed, you are a great teacher and have guided me well. To my friends, Michele Gan, Dyanna Smith, Kim Wilson, Eden DuCrest, and my Aunt Kathy, you all inspire me to be the best I can be. I treasure all of you.

Last but not least, to all my loyal and supportive clients, who motivate me to do what I do, and make each day full of fun and adventure. It has been such a great ride!

Foreword

The phrase "Follow the stars" has always had two meanings for me—the first being get my ass to Hollywood. The second was to find a deeper meaning in my life through astrology. I've become passionate about understanding my destiny and seeking guidance from astrologers and learning how to use dates and celestial influences to improve the quality of my life. Being a Scorpio, well, we tend to have many secrets. I have also learned that in this business, the less you hide the more authentic you can be. That's why when Sabra asked me to open up about our experiences together in a magical cookbook that combined astrology and food I was more than happy to say yes.

I first met Sabra when I went on vacation to Maui five years ago. After cooking one of her insanely delicious meals, she sat down with me to go over my chart. Even though people might suspect it would be easy to guess a celebrity's astrological chart by saying things like "You love being on stage," Sabra didn't guess or even bother to say anything like that. She dove in, past the superficial nonsense, and took a peek into my soul, my inner secrets, and pointed me in the right direction. She went on to tell me how my destiny has to do with my son, Evan, and children's health. She also said that because I am an Aquarius rising, I would surprise many people as to how smart I actually am. I giggled. So did Sabra. She was surprised to discover this about me because she only saw my persona as the funny, fart-blowing, psychotic cheerleader. She kept looking at the chart to make sure that it was accurate.

I told her my image in the public eye was probably going to dramatically change in a few months (this was before I came out publicly about Evan and his autism). She nodded her head and said, "Yes, you are about to come into your power with this Aquarius rising. People are going to look at you much differently from this point on." I smiled and felt relieved; I knew that in a couple months I was going on *Oprah* for the first time to share my story about helping my son to recover from autism. I was hoping the world would take me seriously; and getting confirmation from Sabra's reading made me feel confident my message was going to be heard.

Food was destined to play a huge role in my life. There were digestive issues in my family before I was born, and throughout my life I have struggled to stay healthy. All the while I had this feeling there were more answers out there. Then along came my son, Evan. So, when Sabra had said my destiny had to do with my child and health, I knew she was spot-on.

I had been sharing Evan's story about being diagnosed with autism; it was devastating, but at the same time it caused me to focus all my energy on the research that ultimately helped him to recover. I learned how the foods he was eating altered his behavior, and I was surprised that there were so many studies that proved it—what we consume can trigger mood swings, tiredness, depression, and hold us back from the vitality and joy we deserve. Once I really understood how to eat for my individual needs, my mind became clearer and I had more energy.

But the right foods didn't always have the right taste. I mean, sure, fruits and vegetables and meats are good, but I was craving that orgasm-like feeling of an amazing meal turning on every taste bud and slowly melting in my mouth. Most women would agree that biting into chocolate cake sometimes arouses them more than their husbands in bed! *All* of Sabra's meals have been able to do that for me.

I'm sure you have heard the saying "You are what you eat," but I think that should be changed to "We *feel* what we eat." Sabra Ricci's passion for cooking for Hollywood stars and her lifelong fascination with astrology bring everything together in her truly extraordinary cookbook!

—Jenny McCarthy

Introduction

Some of my warmest memories center on food, as I bet they do for you, too. For me, my favorite meal was Sunday breakfast at my grandparents' house in Sacramento, California. We'd feast on homemade hash browns, smoked ham, maple-cured bacon, and eggs made to order, then sit around laughing and talking. Inevitably my grandfather George would grab a newspaper and read us our "horrible-scopes." Since he and I were both Scorpios, he'd announce whether we had good news ahead or would be better off going back to bed! Thus the connection between food and astrology was born.

My grandpa George was also an experimental and enthusiastic chef—which inspired my career at a very young age. He'd spend hours watching *The Galloping Gourmet* and then rush off to the kitchen to replicate, or in some cases, reinvent, what he had just seen. Whether he was making his own sausage, smoking his own meats, or creating unique breads filled with cheese and salami, he was a pioneer in my world. To this day, in all my travels, I've never tasted lasagna that could compare to Grandpa's.

However, my interest in astrology grew beyond the Sunday horoscope. Throughout my teenage years, I saved all my allowance money to buy books on the subject. I came to view it as an indispensable tool for understanding the human condition—in fact, it's a given that when I meet someone new, I always ask when his or her birthday is.

The third leg of this trilogy of passions, including food and astrology, is entertainment. Ever since my mother dressed me up in my "grown-up girl" clothes (little plaid suit, patent leather Mary Janes, and gloves) to go see *Funny Girl* at the Alhambra Theatre, I've been hooked—on the glitz, the glamour, the excitement. I didn't just want to *see* Barbra Streisand; I wanted to *be* Barbra Streisand.

But it was my passion for food and cooking that eventually led me to culinary school, where I perfected my cooking skills and developed my media persona. I now live in Maui and have had the privilege of working for some of the biggest names in the entertainment industry, which has been a dream come true. While I may not have become the next Barbra Streisand, you never know—Barbra may find herself in need of a personal chef!

Lobster for Leos, Cookies for Capricorns has been a labor

of love in many ways—a love, not just of cooking, but of food, health, astrology, and entertaining. I've designed it according to each of the twelve zodiac signs, incorporating the foods that support the health of the body part ruled by each sign; for example, Gemini rules the lungs, Leo rules the heart, and Libra rules the kidneys. This doesn't mean only one chapter applies to you, however—not at all! You can draw on each of the astrological signs depending on the kind of meal you want to make, the areas of imbalance you want to address, the time of year, or the kind of mood you want to create.

Last, this book has little to do with watching your weight. It's not my intention to tell you what you should or shouldn't eat, but to present you with an array of options for eating naturally, healthfully, seasonally, and in accordance with the stars. You certainly don't have to be an astrology expert to enjoy the book or recipes. The only thing you need is a passion for good food and a sense of adventure. The rest, as they say, is icing on the cake.

Here's to your health, to good friends, and to many, many delicious meals to come.

Much aloha,

Sabra Ricci

Sabra Ricci and Jenny McCarthy.
Courtesy of Robin Layton Photography.

Astrological Guidelines and Definitions

Chances are you know your Sun sign and have probably read your horoscope many times. Maybe you've even had your astrological chart created for you or created it yourself from online software. And if you're really lucky, you've had your chart interpreted by a professional astrologer.

Many consider astrology to be entertainment. Others liken it to a kind of parlor game, with no real meaning. And yet some others are still mystified by it or even view it as a dark art based in superstition. In reality, nothing could be further from the truth. Astrology is a science—an ancient one, dating perhaps as far back as 2300 B.C.E.

Astrology is a science of mathematical calculations using symbols and was used in ancient civilizations—Babylonian, Greek, and Egyptian, to name a few. Symbols have the ability to convey a level of meaning tailored to the comprehension level of the observer. That is why it was so valuable in ancient times. It was respected and practiced by such greats as Socrates, Aristotle, Pythagoras, Nostradamus, and Isaac Newton.

In the 1500s astrology was denounced by the Church. It fell further from favor during the Age of Enlightenment in the eighteenth century. While there were still practitioners throughout the following centuries, astrology's resurgence came in the 1960s with the golden Age of Aquarius and the rise of the "flower children."

Interest in the occult, psychic sciences, and metaphysics soon brought astrology back to the forefront. The advent of the computer and astrology software decades later made it possible for anyone with a computer and some astrological knowledge to set up shop. But a true professional astrologer will have spent many years of study perfecting his or her craft. Many of today's finest astrologers still prefer to use manual mathematical calculations to create their charts by hand, as each chart and person are unique and special. The re-creation of an exact birth chart down to the second can only happen over a 23,000-year period.

ASTROLOGICAL DATES:

ARIES: March 21 – April 19	LIBRA: September 23 – October 22
TAURUS: April 20 – May 20	SCORPIO: October 23 – November 21
GEMINI: May 21 – June 21	SAGITTARIUS: November 22 – December 21
CANCER: June 22 – July 22	CAPRICORN: December 22 – January 19
LEO: July 23 – August 22	AQUARIUS: January 20 – February 18
VIRGO: August 23 – September 22	PISCES: February 19 – March 20

ASTROLOGICAL CHARACTERISTICS:

SIGN	RULER	ENERGY	ELEMENT TRIPLICITY	QUALITY QUADRUPLICITY
ARIES	Mars	Positive	Fire	Cardinal
TAURUS	Venus	Negative	Earth	Fixed
GEMINI	Mercury	Positive	Air	Mutable
CANCER	Moon	Negative	Water	Cardinal
LEO	Sun	Positive	Fire	Fixed
VIRGO	Mercury	Negative	Earth	Mutable
LIBRA	Venus	Positive	Air	Cardinal
SCORPIO	Pluto	Negative	Water	Fixed
SAGITTARIUS	Jupiter	Positive	Fire	Mutable
CAPRICORN	Saturn	Negative	Earth	Cardinal
AQUARIUS	Uranus	Positive	Air	Fixed
PISCES	Neptune	Negative	Water	Mutable

RULER

The ruler is the planet that is said to rule or have charge over the sign. The ruling planets represent the manifestation of what the sign represents in its purest form.

ENERGY

Positive (also called Masculine) and Negative (also called Feminine) refer not to "good" and "bad" but to the kinds of energy associated with that sign. Positive means active energy and negative means passive or receiving energy. The positive signs of the zodiac are action-oriented, outgoing, and extroverted. The negative signs are compliant, reserved, and introverted.

ELEMENT/TRIPLICITY

Elements are characteristics of a person's temperament.

Fire. The fire element is enthusiastic, intuitive, and passionate. Fire runs on gut instinct, is dramatic, and has the ability to lead. The three fire signs, Aries, Leo, and Sagittarius, all share aspects of these characteristics. They burn brightly just like their element.

Earth. The earth element is determined, slow-paced, and "earthy." Earth is sensual, practical, and can be a workaholic. The three earth signs, Taurus, Virgo, and Capricorn, display these characteristics as well as being grounded.

Air. The air element is intellectual, analytical, and flexible. Air is detached, cool, and can appear aloof. The three air signs, Gemini, Libra, and Aquarius, are skilled communicators and very social.

Water. The water element is emotional, sensitive, and has the ability to read people. Water is feeling rather than thinking and has healing abilities. The three water signs, Cancer, Scorpio, and Pisces, possess these characteristics and are also nurturing.

QUALITY/QUADRUPLICITY

Qualities represent periods of time or activities.

Cardinal. Cardinal signs represent beginning, as in the start of a season. In fact, the four cardinal signs begin with the first day of the seasons: Aries, the Spring Equinox (first day of spring); Cancer, the Summer Solstice (first day of summer); Libra, the Vernal Equinox (first day of fall); and Capricorn, the

Winter Solstice (first day of winter). Like the start of a season, cardinal signs get things started and moving. They are the initiators and have great vitality.

Fixed. Fixed signs represent the middle, steady and unchangeable. The middle month of the season is well established. You can rely on the fact that the middle of summer will be hot, the middle of winter will be cold, and so on. The four fixed signs, Taurus, Leo, Scorpio, and Aquarius, are steadfast, resilient, and reliable. They all have strong willpower and an earthy nature.

Mutable. Mutable signs represent dualistic nature and adaptability. The ending of the season is flexible, already edging toward the next new beginning. You will experience changes in the daily temperature as the season prepares to wind down. The four mutable signs, Gemini, Virgo, Sagittarius, and Pisces, are dualistic, changeable, and can adapt to all circumstances life has to offer.

These are just a few of the basics regarding astrology. Many volumes have been written about this subject and I guarantee there will be many more to come. For those who wish to pursue further information or increase your knowledge, please refer to the Resources section (see page 243) for a few of my favorites.

1

Aries

March 21–April 19

BRAINIAC FOODS

All these foods have been carefully selected for Aries, as this sign rules the brain. Aries is the baby of the zodiac, and like any baby, soaks up information like a sponge because of their innate curiosity. They are like the Energizer bunny, constantly on the go. Anytime you need to jump-start a project, Aries is your go-to person.

....

Symbol: Ram
Ruling Planet: Mars
Body Part Ruled: Brain
House Ruled: First, the house of the personality, physical appearance, how others see you

Element: Fire
Color: Red
Stone: Diamond
Key Phrase: I am
Trait: Courage
Quality: Cardinal

Aries being the first sign of the zodiac makes them the most childlike, outgoing, and playful. Some of the best foods for them are the ones that will keep their sassy behavior in line so their creativity can shine. Aries leads the way for all other signs. Just as the brain has dominion over all other body parts, Aries wants to exert that same dominion over the other signs and can stamp their feet like a petulant child when no one else will pay attention or listen to them. But this is just part of the Aries charm, which when they turn it on, can be used to wrap others around their little fingers.

ARIES IN THE KITCHEN

Aries natives possess exuberance in all areas of their lives, which spills over to their love of good food. Like a child digging through their chock-full toy box, playing with each toy and then tossing it aside until the room looks like the latest hurricane has just gone through, an Aries can hit the kitchen in the same manner. Chances are all the pots and pans will be dragged out of the cupboards and the drawers emptied of all the utensils. In fact, the more utilitarian a kitchen is, the better it is for Aries as their curiosity won't get the best of them as they want to try the latest piece of equipment in the middle of preparing dinner. Aries have great pioneering skills and love all the newest gadgets available for the home kitchen. They just need to allow time to read all the directions and become familiar with the capabilities prior to embarking on that special sit-down dinner for their twenty closest friends.

Aries have great creativity and can plan the most successful soiree, but it may take a French brigade to accomplish the finished product. It's good for the Aries "chef" to have a "sous-chef" if possible, as they can easily be distracted when they have too much going on at one time. With the help of someone possessing good organizational skills to do prep work, clean-up, and put all equipment back in place, the Aries will be at their best. Or since Aries are great at starting up projects and leading others, they can create the menu, direct the cooking process, and take the credit for the finished product. But the serious Aries home chef can still aspire to acquiring some of the skills of professional Aries chefs, such as Cat Cora and Ming Tsai.

As a hostess/host, Aries will serve meals with a hint of the exotic, reminiscent of the faraway lands of their childhood storybooks. And they *love* spice! But not to worry, it won't take off the top of your head, it will be just enough to grab your attention. While Aries can be little rebels, it's all for show as a means to get attention and approval. They will definitely want your approval for the meal and will bask in the praise. Should you be disappointed in the fare, the Aries host/hostess will be as embarrassed as a child making a mistake in front of all the other classmates. But they will quickly recover and be on to serving dessert and entertaining their eclectic friends with their quick wit.

ARIES GUESTS

As guests, Aries are gregarious and will liven up your dinner party with their verbal skills. They can be funny, and enjoy socializing with others. They also like attention so you won't find any of your Aries guests sitting in the corner like a wallflower. Instead they will be eager to engage your guests and will keep the conversation flowing.

Be sure to have appetizers ready when the Aries guests arrive with their voracious appetites. Their fiery nature easily depletes their energy and they are apt to be ravenous arriving at your door. Just a few bites will hold them over until dinner is served and pique their interest for what's to come.

Rams delight in the extravagant, so they will appreciate an elaborate table setting, so bring out your beautiful china that you only use occasionally. Vivid red or scarlet are both colors Aries adore so feel free to use either color lavishly in decorating the table, as napkins, tablecloth, or flowers. Be sure to have lots of candles, the more candles the better; they are Cardinal Fire after all!

Don't be afraid of igniting sparks; remember these natives are fearless and creative. They will evacuate everyone, if necessary, to avoid a disaster, rescue the food, grab the tablecloth, spread it on the lawn, and your dinner party will continue while waiting for the fire department to arrive!

FEATURED ARIES BRAINIAC FOODS

All these foods are great for Aries and the brain, but all signs will benefit from the brain-enhancing properties.

Acai Berries. This unique berry has the same antioxidants and vitamins as blackberries and blueberries, but also has protein and omega-3s, making them excellent to keep that Aries brain sharp and quick-witted. Acai berries have quickly been declared a superfood, great for supporting the "super" exuberance possessed by Arians, which often gets them in trouble when their mouths are on overdrive.

Artichokes. This lotus-looking vegetable is high in luteolin, which inhibits brain inflammation by halting the release of the chemical responsible for the aging process of the brain. This asset of artichokes could keep the Aries brain as youthful as their appearance and behavior into their octogenarian years. Of course, hopefully they will have toned down their excitability just a bit so they won't still be jumping up and down to be noticed.

Cacao. The antioxidants in dark chocolate protect the brain. One ounce per day is said to improve concentration and focus due to the natural stimulating substances in chocolate and the increase of endorphins. This will absolutely help Aries stay focused as they lead the charge through life, whether everyone else agrees they are on the right path or not. They are natural leaders, but march to their own drumbeat regardless if others choose to follow or not.

Coffee. Drinking coffee on a regular basis actually can help stem the loss of mental faculties and the risk for Alzheimer's, dementia, and other age-related mental imparities. Of course no sign should overdo coffee consumption—especially high-energy Aries because they need to give their overactive minds a rest once in a while. But there is nothing like a good cup of joe to help an Aries when they are charging full steam ahead to their next conquest, leaving subordinates to wrap up the latest unfinished project.

Matcha. This powder ground from Japanese Gyokuru tea leaves has antioxidants 33 times higher than blueberries. What more could you want to protect the brain? And unlike other tea, you're not discarding the leaves, so Rams will get the full impact. Matcha is a wonderful source of the amino acid L-Theanine, which generates the same effect in calming the mind as Zen Buddhist monks achieve upon meditating for years, making it like an instant tranquilizer for the overactive Aries.

Rosemary. This herb is both antioxidant and anti-inflammatory, known to amplify the functioning of the brain. It is a natural herb choice to prevent swelling from all the overthinking Aries do. Or for those times the Aries needs to think extra hard before blurting out whatever pops into their mind in childlike excitement. For mental acuity, they can regularly add rosemary to their diets and exotic dishes.

Walnuts. These wrinkly brain-shaped nuts are high in vitamin E, which helps decrease memory loss. Called "brain food" by some, this may be due to the theory that if a food resembles a body part, it must be beneficial for it. In this case, it's true. One ounce per day is great for keeping all those cherished Aries memories just a thought away.

Wild Salmon. The emphasis is on "wild" (as opposed to farm-raised, which are shot up with antibiotics). Wild-caught salmon is at the top of the list for having one of the highest concentrations of omega-3 essential fatty acids of any food. This is vital to the brain, which is at least 60 percent fatty tissue. Not to say that Aries are "fatheads," but they are known to think highly of themselves and have a little bit of a "me first" attitude, but like any child this can be endearing.

✳

Acai Berry Smoothie
SERVES 2

Juice is the most well-known form of this great berry. Smoothies are easy to make and great on those busy mornings for people on the go.

> 1 cup Acai berry juice
> 1 banana
> 1 cup plain yogurt (if lactose intolerant or vegan, substitute soy yogurt or almond milk)
> ½ cup freshly squeezed orange juice
> 1 cup crushed ice
> Agave nectar to taste

Add all the ingredients to a blender and, using the smoothie option, if available, blend until smooth and creamy. If needed, add more ice or liquid for the desired consistency.

✳

Double Chocolate Cocoa Nib Cookies

MAKES 6 DOZEN COOKIES

What better way to get a double dose of chocolate? You can pop a couple into a baggie on your way out the door for that afternoon brain boost.

16 tablespoons (2 sticks) butter, at room temperature

¾ cup firmly packed light brown sugar

¾ cup granulated sugar

2 large eggs

1 teaspoon pure vanilla extract

1 teaspoon almond extract

2¼ cups all-purpose flour

¾ cup cocoa powder

1 teaspoon baking soda

½ teaspoon salt

1 cup semisweet chocolate chips

½ cup Dagoba organic cocoa nibs

½ cup almonds, finely chopped

1. Preheat the oven to 350°F. In the bowl of an electric mixer fitted with a paddle attachment, mix the butter, sugars, eggs, vanilla, and almond extract on medium-high speed until light and fluffy.

2. In a separate bowl, blend together the sifted flour, cocoa powder, baking soda, and salt. Add the dry mix to the butter mixture and stir to combine thoroughly. Add the chocolate chips, cocoa nibs, and almonds.

3. Using a 1-ounce ice cream scoop, drop dough balls on ungreased cookie sheets. Bake for 10 to 12 minutes. Cool for 2 minutes on the cookie sheets before transferring to wire racks to finish cooling.

✳

Kona Coffee–Rubbed Flank Steaks with Cilantro-Lime Vinaigrette

SERVES 6

You can have a cup of coffee anywhere, but Kona coffee from exotic Hawaii lends itself to something more substantial. There's nothing like the grilled flavor of this steak.

Rub

¼ cup Kona coffee, espresso grind

2 tablespoons smoked paprika (pimentón)

    2 tablespoons light brown sugar

    2 tablespoons fine Alaea Hawaiian sea salt

    2 tablespoons freshly ground black pepper

    1 tablespoon ancho chili powder

    1 tablespoon garlic powder

    1 tablespoon ground cumin

    1 tablespoon ground coriander

    1 tablespoon toasted ground oregano

    2 pounds flank steak

Vinaigrette

    ½ teaspoon minced fresh ginger

    ½ teaspoon minced fresh garlic

    ½ cup fresh cilantro leaves

    Juice of 2 limes

    ½ teaspoon sea salt

    1 cup olive oil

1. In a bowl, mix together all the spices for the rub. If not using immediately, store in an airtight container.

2. Sprinkle the rub evenly over both sides of the steak and place it in a shallow dish. Cover and refrigerate at least 2 hours or overnight.

3. Add the ginger, garlic, cilantro, lime juice, and salt in the bowl of a food processor and blend until smooth. With the food processor running, add the olive oil in a slow steady stream until the vinaigrette is emulsified. If you prefer a thinner consistency, add a bit of warm water.

4. Preheat a grill to 400°F. Grill the steak for 5 minutes on each side for medium rare. Cover with aluminum foil and let rest on a cutting board for 10 minutes before slicing. Slice thinly on a 45-degree angle across the grain. Drizzle with the vinaigrette and serve.

✳

Artichoke Heart Hummus
SERVES 8

This dish gets to the heart of the situation without all those pesky leaves, allowing you to reap the benefits much sooner.

> 2 cups fresh artichoke hearts, cleaned and cooked
>
> One 14.5-ounce can cannellini beans, drained and rinsed
>
> ½ cup tahini
>
> 3 garlic cloves, minced
>
> Juice of 1 to 2 lemons
>
> 2 teaspoons ground cumin
>
> 1 teaspoon sea salt
>
> ⅓ cup extra-virgin olive oil
>
> Warm water

1. Add the artichokes, cannellini beans, tahini, garlic, lemon juice, cumin, and salt to the bowl of a food processor and blend together, adding the olive oil in a slow steady stream until smooth. Add warm water to reach the desired consistency.

2. Taste the hummus and adjust the seasoning with additional lemon juice and salt if needed. Serve the hummus with warm pita bread and crudités.

Matcha Crème Brûlée

SERVES 6

This treat incorporates your after-dinner cup of tea and dessert into a delightful dish.

> 3 cups heavy cream
> 1 vanilla bean, split and scraped
> 5 large egg yolks
> ¾ cup granulated sugar
> 2 tablespoons matcha green tea powder
> 6 tablespoons Sugar In The Raw

1. Preheat the oven to 325°F.

2. Heat the cream, the scraped vanilla seeds, and the vanilla pod in a heavy-bottomed saucepan over medium-high heat.

Bring to a low boil, then reduce to a simmer. In a mixing bowl, whisk together the egg yolks, the granulated sugar, and the matcha. Add 1 cup of the hot cream mixture to the egg mixture in a slow stream, whisking vigorously, to temper the eggs.

3. Whisk the tempered egg mixture back into the remaining cream mixture in the saucepan and remove from the heat. Remove vanilla pod. Divide the custard equally among six 4-ounce ramekins.

4. Place the ramekins in a roasting pan and fill with water to come halfway up the sides of the ramekins. Bake the custard for 45 minutes, or until set but still a little jiggly in the center. Remove the custard from the roasting pan and let cool. Refrigerate for several hours or up to 2 days.

5. Sprinkle 1 tablespoon of sugar evenly over each custard. Using a blowtorch, melt the sugar until it caramelizes and forms a crisp top. Let cool a few minutes and serve.

*

Panko Rosemary Crusted Rack of Lamb

SERVES 8

Rosemary and lamb is a pairing to tantalize any taste buds. Add crispy panko bread crumbs and parmesan cheese to that crust, and you have a pièce de résistance.

1 tablespoon Montreal Steak Seasoning

1 teaspoon minced garlic

1 tablespoon chopped fresh rosemary

1 teaspoon chopped fresh thyme

¼ cup stone-ground mustard

¼ cup Worcestershire Sauce

¼ cup olive oil

2 racks of lamb, frenched

2 large eggs

1 cup panko bread crumbs

1 cup grated Parmigiano-Reggiano cheese

1. In a small bowl, mix together the Montreal Steak Seasoning, garlic, rosemary, thyme, mustard, Worcestershire, and olive oil. Place the lamb in a shallow container and spread the mixture evenly over the racks of lamb, cover, and place in the refrigerator. Marinate for 24 hours.

2. Preheat the oven to 375°F.

3. Remove the lamb racks from the marinade and pat dry with paper towels. Preheat a large skillet over medium-high heat. Sear the meat on all sides, about 5 minutes. Remove from the heat and let rest until cool enough to handle.

4. In a pan, mix together the panko bread crumbs and Parmigiano-Reggiano cheese. In a separate pan or baking dish, beat the eggs. Dip the seared lamb in the eggs and then dredge in the bread crumb and cheese mixture. Place the lamb in a roasting pan on a baking rack, fat side down, and roast for 20 minutes. Remove from oven and let rest for 10 minutes. Cut into chops and serve.

Wild Salmon on Cedar Planks with Corn and Avocado Salsa

SERVES 6

This is my absolute favorite way to prepare salmon. It is flavorful, easy, and the pairing of salmon and salsa in each bite is heavenly.

Corn and Avocado Salsa
> 2 cups cooked fresh white corn kernels
>
> 2 avocados, peeled, pitted, and diced
>
> Juice of 2 limes
>
> 1 sweet onion, diced
>
> 2 cups grape tomatoes, diced
>
> ¼ cup chopped fresh cilantro
>
> 2 tablespoons olive oil
>
> Sea salt

Salmon
> 1 cedar plank (6 × 14 inches)
>
> 1 side wild salmon, skin and bones removed

¼ cup olive oil

Sea salt and freshly ground black pepper

1. Combine all the ingredients for the salsa in a bowl. Refrigerate the salsa for 1 hour.

2. Soak the cedar plank in water for 20 minutes with a weight on top to keep it submerged. Preheat a grill to medium-high heat.

3. Rinse the salmon and pat dry with paper towels. Brush the soaked plank with oil on both sides. Lay the salmon on the cedar plank, brush with olive oil, and season with salt and pepper to taste. Place the cedar plank in the middle of the grill and cover (the plank will smoke, so keep the lid closed). Cook for 12 to 15 minutes until the salmon is browned but still moist.

4. Fill a squirt bottle with water and have available to extinguish the cinders on the plank. Remove the plank from grill and place on a baking sheet. Transfer the salmon to a platter and serve with the salsa.

Honey Walnut Shrimp

SERVES 8

This recipe is my own healthier adaptation of a hometown favorite. The blending of all the flavors, the crunch of the nuts, and the juicy shrimp are divine.

> 4 tablespoons (½ stick) unsalted butter
>
> 1 cup walnuts
>
> ¼ cup firmly packed brown sugar
>
> 2 cups all-purpose flour
>
> 1 teaspoon salt
>
> 1 cup egg whites
>
> 2 cups extra-fine panko bread crumbs
>
> 2 pounds U-15 shrimp, peeled and deveined
>
> 2 cups canola oil
>
> ¼ cup honey
>
> ½ cup mayonnaise
>
> Juice of 1 lemon
>
> 2 tablespoons sweetened condensed milk

1. In a large sauté pan, melt the butter over medium-high heat. Add the walnuts and stir constantly until toasted, 2 to 3 minutes. Add the sugar and continue stirring until the nuts are coated. Transfer the nuts to a pan lined with parchment paper to cool.

2. Mix the flour and salt together in a pan. In a separate pan or dish, beat the egg whites. Place the panko in a third pan. Dredge the shrimp in the flour, dip in the egg whites, and then into the panko, and coat thoroughly in the bread crumbs. Set the shrimp aside on a baking sheet. Heat the oil over medium-high heat. Line a baking sheet with paper towels. Test cook one shrimp to make sure the oil is hot enough. The shrimp should brown and immediately pop to the surface. Transfer the shrimp to the lined baking sheet. Cook the remaining shrimp. Set aside.

3. Heat the honey, mayonnaise, lemon juice, and condensed milk in a large saucepan, stirring together until bubbly. Arrange the shrimp on platter. Drizzle the sauce over the shrimp and garnish with the candied walnuts.

Taurus

April 20–May 20

MEGAMETABOLIZING FOODS

These foods were selected for Taurus as this sign rules the thyroid. Taurus individuals only need three things to feel truly at home in their own skin: abundance, harmony, and security. And while they don't require loads of material possessions, they must feel comfortable in their surroundings. Luxuriating under an ultrasoft cashmere throw with a couple of down pillows on their cozy bed while sipping hot cocoa is just what they need.

Symbol: Bull
Ruling Planet: Venus
Body Part Ruled: Thyroid
House Ruled: Second, the house of your own resources and values

Element: Earth
Color: Green
Stone: Emerald
Key Phrase: I have
Trait: Dependability
Quality: Fixed

Taurus is the second sign of the zodiac and is determined to achieve all the goals they set. They can be stubborn and will charge full steam ahead like the bull at the matador's cape, only to be surprised sometimes that they should have listened to the guidance of someone with more experience. The thyroid works in conjunction with other organs and body systems, so it is of no surprise that these natives want to have a connection with another person, especially another earth sign, to do almost everything with, walk, talk, eat, laugh . . . anyway, you get the picture.

TAURUS IN THE KITCHEN

Taurus natives have a great love of delectable food, quite possibly more so than any other zodiac sign. They come by this naturally as Taurus also rules the palate, which in any Taurean is very finely tuned. Bulls are, in their own right, superb cooks and adore pairing an excellent meal they have created with the right wine. Most of all it is the outcome that is of importance. As long as everything turns out perfectly, they are happy.

These earth creatures savor the finer things the world has to offer, including their approach to food. When visiting one of your Taurean friends you will never find their fridge empty or their cupboards bare for they like to have the finest-quality comfort foods readily at hand should the mood strike them. Bulls want what they want when they most desire it. Determination is a keynote for the Taurus, and when one makes up his or her mind, nothing, *absolutely nothing,* can change it. So they have learned to have a fully stocked larder rather than trekking out in the middle of the night to satisfy their taste buds.

Taureans love going to the grocery store, making it an event. Perusing the aisles is an adventure for them and they will gladly take you along. This is a natural extension of having their friend by their side. They examine each item before deciding whether it goes back on the shelf or into their basket. You can virtually see them imagining how that new flavor of yogurt would feel and taste on their discriminating palate.

Being an earth sign, the Taurus chef naturally loves the earthy flavors of root vegetables and other things fresh from the garden. It is not unusual for them to keep a little patch of earth ready for a few seeds to grow their own or to have a weekly delivery from a local organic gardener. Is it any wonder that Alice Waters, the pioneer of American cuisine and original sustainable garden chef, is a Taurus?

TAURUS GUESTS

Taurus natives are warmhearted and loving, so make wonderful additions to your guest list. They will easily engage other guests and make them feel welcome and comfortable. Although they can be somewhat self-involved, they rise above it in social settings. In some cases, your Taurus guest will literally entertain people while you are putting the finishing touches on dinner, as some of the world's finest singers just happen to be Taurus.

When inviting a Taurus to dinner, make it an aesthetically appealing event as they love all things beautiful and revel in sumptuous surroundings. This is when they are at their happiest, which is apparent in their behavior and appreciation. This is not to say you must spend a fortune to appease these guests, but just spend a little time planning before setting up the dining room.

Taurus will love to see a sensuous table setting in Venus shades of pale green or pastel shimmery pink as they sit down to the wonderful food you have prepared. They delight in romantic ambiance, soft music, and candles. A centerpiece of violets and pink roses will make this an occasion they will remember. Just make a Taurus feel comfortable and at home, and the evening will be a smashing success.

FEATURED TAURUS MEGAMETABOLIZING FOODS

All these foods are great for Taurus and the thyroid, but all signs will benefit from the properties that keep the metabolism on an even keel.

Arame. These brown seaweed strands are a natural source of trace amounts of iodine needed for proper thyroid function. This plant also has antibiotic and antiviral properties that will assist with those nagging sore throats that can plague any Taurus. A nice seaweed salad on a regular basis will keep the Taurus energy revved up and their throats in tip-top order for crooning the latest tunes.

Brazil Nuts. Brazil nuts are high in selenium and zinc, both of which ensure a healthy thyroid and ample T3 and T4 hormones. Selenium contains enzymes to assist with thyroid detox and hormone production, which maintain the body's energy levels. The benefits of Brazil nuts are especially important for Taurus natives as they have lethargic tendencies due to their love of creature comforts and settling into cozy surroundings.

Celtic Sea Salt. This natural salt contains eighty-four trace minerals, including iodine, zinc, and iron, all necessary for vital thyroid health. It is said to dissipate mucus, which, although it originates in the nose and sinuses, is an irritant to the throat, making this form of salt doubly beneficial and crucial for Taureans who love to express themselves through singing. Many are such melodious songbirds they become singers by profession.

Guava. This yummy fruit is very high in vitamin C (even more so than oranges), and thus promotes healthy cells. It may help boost the thyroid function, helping the body turn food into energy—critical for the Taurus, who are at their best when they can pep up their step.

Mushrooms. Mushrooms are a good source of selenium, but they also contain copper (shiitakes in particular), critical for the production of a thyroid hormone that keeps the formation of cholesterol in check. These earthy fungi are perfect for the earthy Taurus as they are so closely connected to nature. They would delight in a day spent foraging through the forest finding mushrooms for a feast.

Shrimp. Shrimp contains trace amounts of iodine and is very high in vitamin D as well as selenium, iron, and protein. Many people with poor thyroid functioning are deficient in vitamin D, so shrimp can be a double whammy for Taurus with both Vitamin D and iodine. Not to mention they are delighted by the Venusian pink color of perfectly cooked shrimp.

Swiss Chard. Chard is a good secondary source of iodine, and contains plenty of vitamins A, C, and E, all superb antioxidants. This vitamin trio has a neutralizing effect on the trauma and stress that assail anyone on a daily basis, but especially the obstinate Taurus when they are on a stubborn streak. When they make up their minds to push themselves, they will go until they drop. Chard will perk them up until they are reunited with their fluffy pillows.

Wild Rice. This grain isn't rice at all, but marsh grass that has the appearance of rice when cooked. With the high content of B vitamins, folic acid, fiber, and trace amounts of iron, it is a much better grain choice for Taurus. All these benefit the thyroid, aiding in hormone production, cholesterol control, and energy conversion, which will keep Bulls in top performing condition.

*

Arame Napa Cabbage Slaw with Ginger-Sesame Vinaigrette

SERVES 8

A great way to introduce seaweed (like arame and other sea vegetables) into your meals is by combining them with ingredients and tastes with which you are familiar.

Cabbage Slaw

½ head Napa cabbage, cut into chiffonade

¼ head green cabbage

¼ head red cabbage

3 carrots, peeled and shredded

1 hothouse cucumber, seeded and diced

1 cup arame seaweed, reconstituted

Ginger-Sesame Vinaigrette

¼ cup seasoned rice wine vinegar

¼ cup low-sodium tamari

2 tablespoons honey

½ teaspoon minced fresh ginger

½ teaspoon minced fresh garlic

1 tablespoon sesame oil

¼ cup olive oil

2 tablespoons black sesame seeds

1. Mix all the ingredients for the slaw in a medium bowl and toss together.

2. In the bowl of a food processor, add the rice wine vinegar, tamari, honey, ginger, and garlic and turn on the processor. In a slow steady stream, add the sesame oil and olive oil to mixture until it is emulsified.

3. Transfer the dressing from the food processor to a small bowl. Whisk in 1 tablespoon of the black sesame seeds. Toss the dressing with the slaw and mix thoroughly.

4. Chill the slaw for 2 hours. Garnish with the remaining tablespoon of black sesame seeds and serve.

＊

Zucchini Bread with Toasted Brazil Nuts

MAKES 1 LOAF

Brazil nuts are a nice change from the nuts usually added to baked goods, and are excellent with zucchini.

> Organic canola oil spray
> 2 large eggs, beaten
> 1 cup sugar
> ½ cup organic canola oil
> 1 teaspoon pure vanilla extract
> 2 zucchini, shredded
> 1 ½ cups all-purpose flour

1 ½ teaspoons baking soda

1 teaspoon freshly grated nutmeg

1 teaspoon ground cinnamon

½ teaspoon ground cloves

1 cup Brazil nuts, toasted and chopped

1. Preheat the oven to 325°F. Spray a nonstick loaf pan with organic canola oil spray.

2. In the bowl of an electric mixer fitted with the beater attachment, beat the eggs and sugar together on medium-high for 3 minutes until the eggs are pale yellow. Whisk in the vanilla and oil. Stir in the zucchini and set aside.

3. In a bowl, mix together all the dry ingredients, except for the nuts. Gradually mix the dry ingredients into the wet mixture and blend well. Stir in the Brazil nuts, and pour the batter into the prepared loaf pan.

4. Place the pan on the middle rack in the center of the oven and bake for 35 to 40 minutes until golden brown. Test the loaf by inserting a skewer in the center to make sure it is done before removing from oven; the skewer should come out clean. Remove the loaf from the oven and let cool for 10 minutes before removing from the pan.

✳

Celtic Sea Salt Butterscotch Pot de Crème

SERVES 8

Salt enhances the flavors of other ingredients and this is especially true of Celtic sea salt. The sweet, salty, creamy flavors will burst on your tongue and leave you wanting more.

>   3 cups heavy cream
>   1 cup half-and-half
>   8 tablespoons (1 stick) unsalted butter
>   1 cup firmly packed brown sugar
>   1 teaspoon Celtic sea salt
>   6 large egg yolks
>   ¼ cup granulated sugar
>   Pinch of coarse Celtic sea salt for each pot de crème as garnish

1. Preheat the oven to 300°F.

2. In a saucepan, heat 2 cups of the heavy cream and half-and-half until scalding. Remove from the heat.

3. Melt the butter in another saucepan and whisk in the brown sugar and ½ teaspoon of the salt, stirring until smooth.

4. Slowly whisk the cream mixture into the sugar mixture, stirring constantly. Remove from the heat.

5. In a bowl, beat the egg yolks together and add a small amount of the warmed cream mixture, stirring constantly. Add another small amount of the cream mixture to the eggs, repeating the same step. When the eggs are tempered, add the remaining cream mixture and mix together. Divide the custard among eight 4-ounce ramekins.

6. Place the ramekins in a large roasting pan and fill the pan with water to come halfway up the side of each ramekin. Make sure there is an even amount of space between each ramekin. Cover with aluminum foil, place in the middle of the oven and bake for 30 to 40 minutes until set but still a little jiggly in the center. Remove the ramekins from the roasting pan and transfer to a wire rack to cool.

7. Cover and refrigerate the custards for at least 4 hours. Just before serving, using an electric mixer, whip the remaining 1 cup of heavy cream on high speed and add the granulated sugar. Garnish each pot de crème with a pinch of salt and a small dollop of whipped cream.

✳

Coconut-Crusted Onaga (Hawaiian Ruby Snapper) with Guava Sauce

SERVES 4

Coconut, onaga, guava! This is a dish of triple Hawaiian delights. When you taste it, you can easily imagine yourself vacationing on Maui . . .

Onaga

   1 cup all-purpose flour

   ½ teaspoon salt

   1 cup panko bread crumbs

   1 cup shredded fresh coconut

   2 large eggs

   Four 6-ounce onaga fillets, skin and bones removed

   ¼ cup canola oil

Guava Sauce

   5 tablespoons unsalted butter

   1 tablespoon olive oil

   2 tablespoons minced shallot

   ½ cup guava purée (Perfect Purée of Napa Valley)

   ½ cup dry white wine

   1 teaspoon Wondra

   ¼ cup heavy cream

1. Cube 4 tablespoons of the butter and put in the freezer.

2. In a bowl, mix the flour and salt together. In a separate bowl, beat the eggs. In a third bowl mix together the coconut and panko. Dredge the fish in seasoned flour mixture, dip in the egg, and roll in the coconut-panko mixture. Place fish in freezer for a few minutes to set coating.

3. Preheat the oven to 300°F.

4. In a large skillet, heat the oil over medium-high heat. Place the fish in a skillet and cook until golden brown, 2 to 3 minutes on each side. Remove the fish from the skillet and place in a baking dish. Bake in the oven for 15 minutes.

5. In a sauté pan, heat the remaining 1 tablespoon of butter and 1 tablespoon of olive oil over medium-high heat. Add the shallots and sauté for 2 minutes, or until translucent. Add the guava purée and white wine. Bring to a low boil, reduce to a simmer, and cook until the liquid has reduced by half. Remove the frozen butter from the freezer and whisk into the sauce. Sprinkle in the Wondra, stirring constantly; the sauce should start to emulsify. Slowly whisk the cream into the sauce until you reach the desired creamy consistency.

✳

Wild Mushroom Risotto

SERVES 8

Everyone thinks of mashed potatoes and gravy or mac and cheese as comfort foods. But after tasting this risotto, you may just have a new favorite.

6 cups beef stock (or substitute chicken or mushroom stock)

3 tablespoons olive oil

2 tablespoons butter

1 cup shiitake mushrooms, stemmed and julienned

1 cup oyster mushrooms, sliced

1 cup cremini mushrooms, sliced

Salt and freshly ground black pepper

½ cup finely chopped shallots

1 pound Principato di Lucedio Arborio rice

½ cup Courvoisier cognac

½ cup heavy cream

½ cup grated Parmigiano-Reggiano cheese

¼ cup chopped flat-leaf parsley

1. Pour the stock into a stockpot and bring to a boil. Reduce to a simmer.

2. In a medium sauté pan, heat 1 tablespoon of the olive oil and 1 tablespoon of the butter over medium-high heat. Add the mushrooms and sauté for 5 minutes, or until tender. Season with salt and pepper to taste. Remove from the heat and set aside.

3. Heat the remaining olive oil and butter in a heavy-bottomed pot over medium-high heat. Add the shallots and sauté until translucent. Add the rice and cook, stirring constantly, until golden brown. Pour in the cognac and keep stirring until it is completely absorbed. Using a large ladle, add the stock one ladle at a time, stirring constantly, until absorbed. Continue this process until all the stock is used and the rice is creamy.

4. Add the mushroom mixture to the risotto and continue cooking and stirring. Stir in the heavy cream and cheese and continue stirring. Risotto should have a very creamy texture. Season with salt and pepper to taste. Serve immediately, garnished with chopped parsley.

✳

Spicy Shrimp with Hearts of Romaine and Creamy Avocado Dressing
SERVES 4

This delicious salad combines the five tastes: bitter (romaine), sour (lemon, lime juices), sweet (brown sugar, shrimp), salty (salt, Worcestershire sauce), and umami/savory (cheese), making this a dish to tantalize all the taste buds with each bite.

Croutons

1 tablespoon olive oil

1 tablespoon unsalted butter

1 8 × 8-inch square cornbread, cubed

Sea salt

2 tablespoons grated Parmigiano-Reggiano cheese

Spicy Shrimp

1 teaspoon smoked paprika (pimentón)

1 teaspoon ground cumin

Pinch of cayenne pepper

1 tablespoon brown sugar

½ teaspoon salt

Juice of 2 limes

¼ cup olive oil

2 tablespoons chopped fresh cilantro

20 large shrimp, peeled and deveined

Hearts of Romaine

2 hearts of romaine, washed and dried (leave in whole leaves)

½ cup shaved Parmigiano-Reggiano cheese

Creamy Avocado Dressing

1 egg, coddled

Juice of ½ lemon

1 teaspoon minced garlic

1 tablespoon Worcestershire Sauce

½ teaspoon Tabasco sauce

1 tablespoon Dijon mustard

1 cup olive oil

1 avocado, peeled, pitted, and chopped

Salt and freshly ground black pepper

1. Preheat the oven to 300°F.

2. In a large skillet, heat the oil and butter over medium-high heat. Add the cubed cornbread to the pan and brown evenly. Remove from heat and toss with salt and the grated cheese.

3. Spread the cubes out evenly on a sheet pan and bake in the oven until crispy, 10 to 15 minutes. Remove from the oven and let cool. Store in an airtight container until ready to use.

4. In a mixing bowl, combine all the ingredients for the shrimp together except for the shrimp and mix thoroughly. Add the shrimp, toss, and refrigerate for 2 hours maximum.

5. To the bowl of a food processor, add the coddled egg, lemon juice, garlic, Worcestershire, Tabasco, and Dijon, and blend together until smooth. Slowly add olive oil in a steady stream until the mixture is emulsified. Add the avocado and blend until smooth. Use a small amount of warm water to thin out the dressing to the right consistency, if needed. Season with salt and pepper to taste.

6. Preheat a grill to medium-high heat. Grill the shrimp 2 minutes on each side, or until firm. Remove from the heat and cover with aluminum foil.

7. Toss the romaine leaves with the dressing and some of the croutons. Assemble on individual serving plates; top with the remaining croutons and the shaved Parmesan. Arrange 5 shrimp around the outside of each plate, and serve.

✳

Warm Swiss Chard and Portobello Salad with Pancetta

SERVES 4

Swiss chard is my all-time favorite green! It grew in our back-yard growing up and came back every year, and I snipped a few leaves every day all summer. And who doesn't love meaty, rich portobellos?

Salad

>   5 ounces pancetta, diced
>   1 tablespoon olive oil
>   1 tablespoon unsalted butter
>   3 garlic cloves, minced
>   1 large red onion, cut into thin half-moons
>   ½ pound portobello mushrooms, stemmed and cut into strips
>   1 large bunch red Swiss chard, washed and chopped
>   1 cup chicken stock

Mustard Vinaigrette

>   1 teaspoon Coleman's dry mustard
>   2 tablespoons agave nectar
>   2 tablespoons red wine vinegar
>   ¼ cup olive oil

1. Heat a large sauté pan over medium-high heat, add the pancetta and sauté until browned and crisp. Remove the pancetta from the pan, transfer to paper towels, and set aside, leaving the fat in the pan.

2. Add the olive oil and butter to the fat in the pan and place over medium-high heat. Add the garlic and onions and sauté until the onions are translucent, 2 to 3 minutes. Add the mushrooms and Swiss chard and sauté, adding small amounts of chicken stock, as needed, and stirring constantly, until tender.

3. In a small bowl, mix together the dry mustard, agave nectar, and red wine vinegar and stir until smooth. Whisk in the olive oil until emulsified. Add half of the pancetta to the vinaigrette and toss with warm Swiss chard. Serve warm, garnished with the remaining pancetta.

Butternut Squash and Wild Rice Pilaf

SERVES 8

Wild rice was abundant when I was growing up. I came to love the nutty flavor and use it in many recipes instead of white or brown rice. This is a favorite.

2 cups peeled and diced butternut squash

3 tablespoons olive oil

Pinch of sea salt

1 tablespoon unsalted butter

2 garlic cloves, minced

1 cup diced yellow onion

½ cup diced celery

½ cup diced carrot

1 teaspoon chopped fresh thyme

1 cup wild rice

2 ½ cups chicken stock

½ cup dry sherry

1 cup pecans, toasted and chopped

1. Preheat the oven to 400°F.

2. Toss the butternut squash with 2 tablespoons of the olive oil and the salt. Spread the squash out evenly on a baking sheet and roast in the preheated oven for approximately 30 minutes, or until browned. Remove from the oven and set aside.

3. Heat the remaining tablespoon of olive oil and the butter in a sauté pan over medium-high heat. Add the garlic, onion, celery, and carrots and sauté for 3 minutes. Season with thyme and sea salt and set aside.

4. Rinse the wild rice several times in cold water. Add the wild rice, chicken stock, sherry, and vegetable mixture to a small rice cooker and set on auto-cook.

5. When the rice is cooked, transfer it to a serving bowl and stir in butternut squash and pecans. This is a great side dish for roasted chicken or turkey.

3
Gemini

May 21–June 21

EASY-BREATHING FOODS

These foods were chosen for Gemini, ruler of the lungs, renowned for their gift of gab and impeccable communication skills. Gemini natives must include foods in their diets to keep the breath of life flowing and be able to converse throughout their lives. Losing the ability for powerful communication would be a death sentence for Gemini as there is absolutely nothing they would rather do.

Symbol: The Twins
Ruling Planet: Mercury
Body Part Ruled: Lungs
House Ruled: Third, the house of communication
Element: Air

Color: Yellow
Stone: Agate
Key Phrase: I think
Trait: Responsiveness
Quality: Mutable

Gemini rules the house of all communications, along with the ruling planet Mercury, named for the messenger god, moving across the Heavens at lightning speed to deliver the latest tidings. The mind of Gemini moves with that same ultraspeed. They're both excellent communicators and coveted guests at any social gathering. They would rather spend a lifetime gathering knowledge to share with others than obtaining material possessions or wealth. Geminis are such gifted speakers that even if their information isn't completely accurate, they will soon have you hanging on every word, believing it to be gospel.

GEMINI IN THE KITCHEN

All Geminis love conversing and interacting with anyone, whereas other signs feel more comfortable carrying on lively conversations with their friends. Geminis *love* talking to anyone and will banter with a stranger on the street to fulfill their need to speak. This obsession with communication can almost be their downfall as they can quite easily forgo eating and they would much prefer to be out socializing than being in the kitchen with the mundane task of preparing their own meals.

The Gemini communication skills also carry over into sharing experiences and teaching, so they do best in the kitchen when they have an audience. They like anything that can be prepared quickly and become impatient if they have to wait too long. So having their guests gathered around them in the kitchen will help keep the focus off how long it is taking for the roast chicken to finish—the whole cooking experience feels like a social event to them.

The Gemini mind flits from one thing to another like a hummingbird flies through the flowerbed at lightning speed, but unlike other signs, Geminis can focus on many ideas at once. Other signs could consider this unorthodox cooking style to be a distraction, but Gemini draws strength from the interaction, building on each exchange, and finally culminating with more lively dialogue while sharing the meal.

Like professional chef Jamie Oliver, who brings the audience along from his trek through his garden, gathering what he will prepare, to sharing the complete meal on screen, as if everyone were right there with him, so does the Gemini home chef revel in the accomplishment.

GEMINI GUESTS

When you have your Gemini friends on the guest list, you need to keep several things in mind. These creatures are high energy; with the symbol of the Twins it is possible for one Gemini to possess the energy of two. When left to their own devices, they will always eat while watching the latest new DVD or reading the newest bestseller, so you definitely have to grab their attention and keep it.

They love exotic diverse foods that will pique their interest and their appetites, but will completely lose interest if they have to wait between courses. You can keep them entertained with lively conversation, musical interludes, or other forms of entertainment. This is not to say that the Gemini native is picky or difficult as a dinner guest; they're intrigued by the unusual, so mix it up with different spices and out-of-the-ordinary side dishes to accompany the main course. The fact that Mahi Mahi is a good protein source for the Twins should give you a clue.

Have a couple of extroverts in the group and Geminis will be happy, as their wit and charm will win over anyone. Even if they should become slightly bored, you probably won't notice as they are naturally born with social graces and manners.

Geminis love natural ambiance, reminiscent of fields, forests, and mountains, where they feel completely at peace. You certainly don't have to spend a fortune turning your home into a forest sanctuary. But if the season is appropriate, set a lovely table on your patio with napkins in shades of pale yellow, where the Gemini can relax in nature. If that isn't possible, decorate your dining room table with bouquets of field flowers and bring nature inside.

FEATURED GEMINI EASY-BREATHING FOODS

All these foods are great for Gemini and the lungs, but all signs will benefit from clearer, stronger lungs.

Brussels Sprouts. Brussels sprouts are high in folate, dietary fiber, vitamin K, and minerals for optimum health. They also are high in vitamins A and C, the antioxidants with anti-inflammatory properties that help asthma and the inflammation associated with the disease. Any Gemini should make these miniature cabbages an addition to their diet often to keep them breathing easy.

Cannellini Beans. Loaded with magnesium, folate, dietary fiber, and the anti-inflammatory copper, these beans are highly beneficial for lung health, especially for the asthma prone. They also contain nutrients responsible for body detoxification to reduce lung inflammation. The intellectual Gemini needs all their lung power for their next important discourse.

Cantaloupe. This juicy melon promotes healthy lungs with its high content of antioxidant vitamins A and C. It reduces inflammation and is an emphysema preventative, making it a good fruit choice for Gemini whose lungs must be in tip-top shape to hold the massive amounts of air they need to get through the day. Of course cantaloupe is also great for all other signs.

Cornmeal. Cornmeal is high in magnesium, zinc, vitamins B, C, and E, and all cancer inhibitors, plus the antioxidant properties can also benefit those with asthma. Gemini and other signs should definitely include cornbread, corn tortillas, or other corn products on their shopping lists.

Mahi Mahi. Rich in selenium, niacin, B vitamins, and minerals, this cold-water fish protects against emphysema and other lung inflammations, making this an excellent choice for smokers or those exposed to secondhand smoke. It is a great option for the very social Geminis who are often subjected to these pollutants when they are out and about.

Oregano. Packed with iron, manganese, and vitamin C, and a good source of vitamin A, oregano is a key for lung health. Some research suggests vitamin A may support the healing of lung tissue, great news for Gemini or other signs suffering from lung issues. With their tendency toward frustration when they aren't at the top of their game, oregano on a daily basis will help keep any Gemini healthy.

Raspberries. Diets high in vegetables and fruit have been shown to protect against diseases of the lungs, such as COPD (chronic obstructive pulmonary disease). Raspberries are a good choice for this purpose with their high vitamin C content, folate, iron, and potassium, and may also ease other lung issues that may plague Geminis.

Thyme. The volatile oils in thyme are antibacterial and antimicrobial, providing excellent defense against infections of the lungs, bronchial passages, and the entire respiratory system. Iron and manganese provide Geminis protection against free radicals. It is punishment of the cruel and unusual variety for a Gemini to be without their voice, so thyme should definitely be their herb of choice.

✳

Marinated Roasted Brussels Sprouts
SERVES 8

My daughter was probably one of the rare kids growing up who loved Brussels sprouts. They are still one of her favorites, especially roasted.

Salt

2 pounds Brussels sprouts, trimmed

1 teaspoon minced garlic

1 tablespoon minced shallots

¼ cup freshly squeezed lemon juice

1 teaspoon dried oregano

1 teaspoon sea salt

1 cup olive oil

Parmigiano-Reggiano cheese

1. Bring a large pot of water to a boil with salt.

2. Fill a bowl with ice and cover with water. Add the Brussels sprouts to the pot of boiling water and blanch for 5 minutes. Drain and immediately plunge into the ice bath until cool. Drain and let sit in the colander for 10 minutes.

3. In a large bowl, mix together the remaining ingredients. Toss the Brussels sprouts with the marinade until thoroughly coated. Place in the refrigerator and marinate overnight or up to 24 hours.

4. Preheat the oven to 400°F.

5. Remove the Brussels sprouts from the refrigerator and pour into a colander and drain. Transfer from the colander to a rimmed baking sheet. Roast in oven for 20 to 25 minutes until brown and crispy. Remove from oven and, using a Microplane grater, grate Parmigiano-Reggiano to taste over the top. Serve immediately.

✳

Cannellini Bean Ragout with Grilled Rosemary Shrimp

SERVES 8

Cannellini beans have always been a family favorite. This ragout is the perfect accompaniment to the rosemary-scented shrimp.

Beans

> 1 pound dry cannellini beans, rinsed
>
> 6 cups water
>
> 3 garlic cloves
>
> 1 onion, diced
>
> 1 bay leaf
>
> Parsley stems
>
> Salt

Shrimp Skewers

> Thirty-two U-15 shrimp, peeled and deveined
>
> 1 teaspoon minced garlic
>
> 1 tablespoon lemon pepper seasoning
>
> ¼ cup olive oil
>
> 16 rosemary skewers, leaves removed from the bottom half
>   of the stem

Ragout

> *Cooked cannellini beans*
>
> *Salt*
>
> *2 cups fresh tomato, seeded and diced*
>
> *Zest of 1 lemon*
>
> *2 tablespoons freshly squeezed lemon juice*
>
> *1 tablespoon finely chopped fresh rosemary*
>
> *¼ cup extra-virgin olive oil*
>
> *1 lemon, cut into 8 wedges for serving*

1. In a large bowl, cover the cannellini beans with cold water and let soak overnight.

2. The next day, drain and rinse the beans. In a large pot, cover the beans with 6 cups of water. Add the garlic, onion, bay leaf, and parsley stems and bring to a boil. Reduce the heat and simmer until the beans are tender, about 1 hour. Remove the bay leaf. Season with salt and let cool for 20 minutes.

3. In a large bowl, mix the shrimp with the garlic, lemon pepper, and olive oil until the shrimp are coated. Hook two shrimp so they are intertwined and skewer with a rosemary stem. Repeat with the remaining shrimp and refrigerate the skewers.

4. Transfer the cannellini beans to a bowl. Add the tomato, lemon zest, lemon juice, chopped rosemary, and olive oil and toss together. Set the ragout aside.

5. Preheat a grill to medium-high heat.

6. Remove the shrimp from the refrigerator. Spray the grill with nonstick cooking spray. Place the shrimp on the grill so the rosemary end is not in the direct flame and grill the shrimp for 2 minutes on each side. Transfer the shrimp to a pan or baking sheet on the top rack of the grill to keep them warm while cooking the remaining shrimp.

7. On a large platter, spread bean ragout out evenly. Arrange the shrimp skewers on top of the beans, garnish with the lemon wedges, and serve.

✳

Grilled Mahi Mahi with Orange and Ginger Beurre Blanc

SERVES 4

Mahi Mahi is the most popular fish in Hawaii and this preparation is a favorite of my clients from all over the world. So whether you're a Gemini, or you just want to bring a little "Aloha" into your dining experience, this is sure to be a big hit.

Beurre Blanc

  ½ tablespoon olive oil

  1 ½ teaspoons unsalted butter plus 4 tablespoons
      (½ stick) cut into small pieces and placed in freezer

  2 tablespoons minced shallot

2 tablespoons minced fresh ginger

1 cup freshly squeezed orange juice

1 tablespoon Wondra

¼ cup heavy cream

Mahi Mahi

Four 5-ounce Mahi Mahi fillets

Salt and freshly ground black pepper

1. Preheat the oven to 300°F and a grill to 375°F. Season the fish with salt and pepper to taste. Mark the fish on the grill on both sides, for about 5 minutes. Remove the fish from the grill and transfer to a baking dish and cover with aluminum foil. Place in the oven for 10 minutes.

2. In a sauté pan, heat the olive oil and the 1½ teaspoons butter over medium-high heat. Add the shallots and ginger and sauté until the shallots are translucent, about 2 minutes. Add the orange juice and bring to a low boil, reduce the heat, and simmer until the orange juice is reduced by half. Add the frozen butter pieces and sprinkle Wondra over the butter and whisk together until the butter is melted and the consistency is creamy. Finish the sauce by whisking in the heavy cream.

3. Serve the fish immediately with the beurre blanc sauce.

✳

Cantaloupe, Tomato, and Basil Salad with Feta Cheese

SERVES 4

We always had fresh tomatoes and cantaloupes from nearby farms when I was a kid. This salad is a unique way to combine two great flavors.

1 cantaloupe, halved and seeded

½ red onion, peeled, halved, and sliced into thin half-moons

1 pint red teardrop tomatoes, cut in half lengthwise

¾ cup fresh basil leaves, cut into chiffonade

¼ cup Villa Manodori balsamic vinegar

¼ cup extra-virgin olive oil

Sea salt

4 ounces French feta cheese, crumbled

1. Using a melon baller, scoop melon balls into a large bowl. Add the onion, tomato, and ½ cup of the basil and mix together.

2. In a small mixing bowl, whisk together the vinegar, olive oil, and salt.

3. Transfer the melon and tomato mixture to a serving bowl. Drizzle the vinaigrette over salad. Garnish with the remaining ¼ cup basil and the crumbled feta.

✳

Cornmeal Pancakes with Blueberries and Sour Cream

SERVES 8

Cornmeal pancakes are a nice alternative to other breakfast fare. You get the tastes of cornbread and buttermilk pancakes rolled into one delicious dish.

1 cup unbleached all-purpose flour

1 cup yellow cornmeal

1 teaspoon baking powder

1 teaspoon baking soda

½ teaspoon salt

1½ cups buttermilk

¼ cup honey

3 large eggs

¼ cup vegetable oil

2 cups light sour cream

½ cup firmly packed brown sugar

1 pint blueberries

1. Preheat the oven to 200°F.

2. In a bowl, sift together the dry ingredients and set aside.

3. In another bowl, whisk together the buttermilk, honey, eggs, and oil. Slowly pour the wet mixture into the dry mixture, stirring constantly. Pour the batter into a quart-size measuring pitcher.

4. Preheat a large griddle to medium-high heat.

5. Spray the griddle with nonstick canola oil cooking spray. Pour out enough batter for four large pancakes, using about half of the batter. When the pancakes get little bubbles all over, flip and cook the other side. The pancakes should be golden brown on both sides. Transfer the pancakes to a baking dish and place in the oven to keep them warm. Repeat, making pancakes with the remaining batter.

6. In a small mixing bowl, whisk together the sour cream and brown sugar until the sugar dissolves.

7. Serve the pancakes topped with the sweetened sour cream and the blueberries.

Cucumber-Tomato Salad with Fresh Oregano

SERVES 8

This is one of my favorite salads for summer. When I was growing up, we always had a garden, overflowing with cucumbers and tomatoes. This was a quick, easy, and delicious salad that was a staple on our table.

4 cucumbers, peeled and sliced

4 large vine-ripened tomatoes, cored and cut into eight
wedges

1 red onion, peeled, halved, and sliced in thin half-moons

1 teaspoon Dijon mustard

1 teaspoon minced garlic

3 tablespoons finely chopped fresh oregano

¼ cup red wine vinegar

1 tablespoon agave nectar

½ cup olive oil

Sea salt and freshly ground black pepper

1. In a large salad bowl, mix together the first three ingredients and set aside.

2. In a small mixing bowl, whisk together the Dijon mustard, garlic, oregano, red wine vinegar, and agave nectar. Slowly whisk in the olive oil. Season with salt and pepper to taste.

3. Toss the vegetable mixture with the vinaigrette, cover, and refrigerate for at least 2 hours before serving.

✳

Panna Cotta with Raspberry Purée

SERVES 8

Nothing is better than raspberries and cream. This is the ultimate!

Panna Cotta

1 envelope gelatin

2 tablespoons water

2½ cups heavy cream

1½ cups half-and-half

½ cup sugar

1 vanilla bean

Mint sprigs for garnish

Raspberry Purée

3 pints raspberries

¾ cup sugar

1 tablespoon freshly squeezed orange juice

1 tablespoon Grand Marnier

1. In a medium bowl, stir the gelatin and water together and set aside to dissolve.

2. In a medium saucepan, mix the heavy cream, half-and-half, and sugar over medium-high heat. Cut the vanilla bean lengthwise and scrape out the seeds with the back of a knife and add to the cream mixture along with the pod. Bring the mixture to a low boil and turn off the heat. Remove the vanilla pod and pour into a bowl, add the gelatin mixture, and whisk together.

3. Spray eight 4-ounce ramekins with nonstick cooking spray. Pour the cream mixture into the ramekins and let sit for 10 minutes to cool. Cover and place in the refrigerator for at least 4 hours or overnight.

4. In a food processor, purée 2 pints of the raspberries, the sugar, orange juice, and Grand Marnier. Pour the mixture through a fine-mesh sieve or cheesecloth to remove the seeds. Chill the purée for at least 2 hours before serving.

5. To serve, run a table knife around the inside edge of each ramekin until the panna cotta starts to pull away from the edge. Invert each one onto a small individual serving dish. Ladle the raspberry purée over each panna cotta and garnish with the remaining pint of fresh raspberries and a mint sprig.

Thyme and Panko Crusted Chicken Milanese

SERVES 4

Milanese style is one of my favorite ways to prepare chicken. And I love it with the spicy bite of the arugula!

4 boneless, skinless chicken breasts

1 cup all-purpose flour

Salt and freshly ground black pepper

2 large eggs

1 tablespoon chopped fresh thyme

½ cup grated Parmigiano-Reggiano cheese

1 ½ cups panko bread crumbs

Vegetable oil

4 cups baby arugula

Extra-virgin olive oil

2 cups diced vine-ripened tomato

Shaved Parmigiano-Reggiano cheese for garnish

2 lemons, cut into 8 wedges

1. Cut the chicken breasts in half lengthwise. Place four pieces of chicken into two large ziplock bags, close, squeezing out all the air. Using a mallet or meat pounder, pound the chicken out on both sides until ¼ to ½ inch thick. Set aside.
2. Pour the flour into a pan and season with salt and pepper to taste. In another pan or dish, beat the eggs. In a separate

pan, mix together the thyme, grated cheese, and panko bread crumbs. Dredge the pieces of chicken one at a time in the seasoned flour, then dip in the beaten egg mixture, and then dredge in the panko bread crumb mixture until coated. Place the chicken on a baking sheet, using wax paper sheets to layer. Refrigerate for 30 minutes.

3. Preheat the oven to 300°F.

4. In a large sauté pan, heat the vegetable oil over medium-high heat. Add the chicken and sauté until golden brown on each side. Transfer to a plate with paper towels to absorb excess oil. Transfer to a pan and place in the oven until ready to serve.

5. In a medium bowl, toss the arugula with the extra-virgin olive oil and season with salt. Divide the arugula equally among four plates. Arrange two pieces of chicken on each plate and top with the diced tomatoes. Garnish with the lemon wedges and shavings of parmesan.

4 Cancer

June 22–July 22

TUMMY-SOOTHING FOODS

These Cancer selections are great for the tummy and the entire digestive system. Nothing can waylay a person like an upset stomach or sluggish digestion. Cancer can benefit from these foods to avoid uncomfortable and often embarrassing digestive issues. They know all about nurturing, comforting, and making everyone feel better, so it is only natural Cancer rules the tummy.

....

Symbol: Crab
Ruling Planet: Moon
Body Part Ruled: Stomach
House Ruled: Fourth, the house of the home
Element: Water

Color: Gray
Stone: Pearl
Key Phrase: I feel
Trait: Loyalty
Quality: Cardinal

Cancer and its ruling planet the moon rule the fourth house, the house of the home. The moon and Cancer also rule the stomach, the appetite, and the whole digestive process—including how nutrition is absorbed. The array of emotions affecting a Cancer on a daily basis can cause sensitive digestion, but also gives them sensitivity for the emotional makeup of all other signs.

The moon represents the mother and rules the emotions. Cancer is the great nurturer of the zodiac and embodies the full range of emotions motherhood entails, whether you're a mother or not: sympathy and compassion, tenderness, and the forcefulness of a mother bear protecting her cubs. Beware—threaten the Cancerian family and feel the pinch of the crab's powerful claws!

CANCER IN THE KITCHEN

Cancer is expert at providing emotional support and desires security and comfort in return. The adage "A man's home is his castle" is true of this sign more than any other, whether male or female. They are quite domestic, albeit not always the best at housekeeping, and have a knack of making anyone feel at home. In fact, if they have no immediate family of their own, they will soon "adopt" friends to nurture. If you are fortunate enough to receive an invitation to their home for any occasion, be it only tea and cookies, it will be prepared with such love and thoughtfulness, you will instantly feel like a member of the family.

Cancer is the most sensitive sign of the zodiac and those under this sign are said to feel the pain of others, which contributes to their nurturing capabilities. No other sign knows how to "mother" someone like Cancer. They have a natural ability of knowing when to back off in order not to be smothering. This carries over into the kitchen, where they can intuitively know what to prepare for each guest without knowing their favorite foods.

Crabs are great lovers of food. These natural gastronomes love the kitchen and feel more at home there than in any other room of the house! They may be more comfortable around a stove than any other sign. Nothing pleases them more than to prepare a wonderful meal for family and friends; in fact, it may just possibly put them "over the moon." They have a knack for making anyone feel at home in their presence and relish in the sheer delight of watching contented friends, sated with scrumptious foods.

And to close the evening, you may find yourself leaving with your favorite antique trinket box from the Cancer's personal collection, just because you mentioned you loved it.

They love to share their possessions with their loved ones, and newly adopted friends qualify.

CANCER GUESTS

Cancer natives have very defined emotional systems, and are extremely sensitive to their environment, their surroundings, and the people in their lives. They use their own sensitivity to relate to others, establish rapport, and gain understanding of others. Secure within themselves, Crabs can develop heightened intuition, which will benefit themselves and how they interact with others, making them an ideal guest.

Cancers are known for their variable nature, but when it comes to accepting invitations, your Cancer friends will be enchanting, charming guests. If you wish to woo your Cancer guest, serve a delicious feast prepared just for them to whet their great appetites. This will be a close second to the pleasure they feel at preparing the meal themselves. They delight in flavors that are sweet and pungent, which if prepared for them with loving care, will have an endearing effect. Pair the entrée with a complementing wine and you will have a very appreciative Cancer on your hands as they are always happiest after a delicious meal.

Their imaginations are heightened by fine linens in pale hues of yellow and orange. Fragrances of roses wafting above the silvery lunar candlelight will make a heady atmosphere, which welcomes Cancer and makes them feel at home. Make this a memorable night and you will find yourself taken in by these creative sensitive creatures.

FEATURED CANCER TUMMY-SOOTHING FOODS

All these foods are great for Cancer, the stomach, and digestion, but all signs will benefit from the properties that keep that food moving.

Buckwheat. High in fiber and amino acids, buckwheat gets things moving through the digestive tract and promotes the growth of probiotics (healthy bacteria in the gut), keeping the whole system in great shape. Buckwheat has many wonderful properties that benefit the entire body, but it all starts in the stomach and buckwheat is excellent for the metabolism of all systems. It also makes a great breakfast.

Fennel. Another superfood, fennel has long been used to ease problems of the digestive system. While you may have eaten a few of the seeds as you leave an Indian restaurant, the bulb and leaves of the fennel plant also have medicinal properties. It is an appetite stimulant, and its antispasmodic properties can soothe an upset stomach. It also aids in the oxidation of fatty foods. Cancers should try more than just the seeds, as not only will they feel better, they will have new recipes to share with the family.

Green Tea. Green tea is a powerhouse: it revs up digestion, helping your body break down food, soothes an upset stomach, and may even combat food poisoning. Cancers might enjoy breaking out a special antique teacup to enjoy some after dinner each night, and anyone else who wishes to ease digestion.

Leeks. High in vitamins A, C, and K and dietary fiber, leeks boost the digestion process and strengthen the entire digestive tract, making them a healthy choice. Leeks activate the release of enzymes by the pancreas, stimulating digestion. A nice bowl of leek soup or a side of sautéed leeks can promote digestive health for all signs.

Pineapple. Pineapple contains vitamins A and C, bromelain, and other enzymes that greatly benefit the digestive system. Slices of fresh pineapple after each meal will enhance the whole digestive process. The touchy Cancer stomach will appreciate soothing. Anti-inflammatory properties reduce swelling and alleviate pain. Take a cue from Crabs and have your daily dose of fresh pineapple or sip the golden juice.

Radishes. Radishes stimulate digestion, aid with liver health, and activate the flow of bile with sulfur compounds. Black radishes are especially helpful in eradicating mucus throughout the digestive tract. All signs can benefit from keeping these little gems in the fridge as a healthy snack, but Cancers should definitely indulge. Those high emotions could just cause the Crab a case of indigestion, and the accompanying crankiness doesn't serve these nurturers.

Watercress. Having a watercress salad before the entrée can prevent indigestion. It is also highly beneficial for the gallbladder, which stores all that bile. While great for Cancer natives, all other signs should try this peppery green to keep the digestive system moving along.

Watermelon. Juicy, sweet, and fun to eat off the rind (and spit seeds at each other), watermelon is one of the great all-time treats mothers serve their children. And it's also good for you! Used from ancient times to boost sluggishness, it aids indigestion, and is even higher than tomatoes in lycopene, a powerhouse antioxidant against free radicals.

*

Chilled Soba Noodle Salad with Tofu and Sesame Vinaigrette

SERVES 6

Great cool salad on a sultry day!

Salad

14 ounces soba noodles, cooked and drained

2 cups snow peas, trimmed, blanched, and cut thinly on the diagonal

1 cup baby corn, cut in quarter pieces

½ cup scallions, trimmed and cut thinly on the diagonal

1 carrot, peeled and julienned

Small red bell pepper, seeds and membranes removed, julienned

8 ounces extra-firm tofu, cut into small cubes

Sesame Vinaigrette

1 teaspoon minced garlic

2 teaspoons minced ginger

¼ cup low-sodium tamari sauce

¼ cup seasoned rice vinegar

2 tablespoons honey

1 tablespoon sesame oil

¼ cup olive oil

¼ cup toasted sesame seeds

1. In a large bowl, mix the salad ingredients together.

2. Whisk together the garlic, ginger, tamari, rice vinegar, and honey in a small mixing bowl. Slowly add the sesame and olive oils, whisking constantly.

3. Drizzle the vinaigrette over the noodles and vegetables and toss thoroughly. Garnish with the sesame seeds.

＊

Green Tea, Pineapple, and Ginger Martini for Two

MAKES 2 MARTINIS

Sheer bliss, and good for you, too!

> 1 teaspoon fresh chopped ginger
>
> 6 ounces premium vodka
>
> 4 ounces green tea
>
> 2 ounces fresh pineapple juice
>
> 2 skewers of fresh pineapple chunks

1. Muddle the ginger with the vodka and green tea. Add the pineapple juice and fill a shaker with ice.

2. Shake, shake, shake, and strain the martini into two chilled glasses. Garnish with the pineapple skewers.

✳

Shaved Fennel, Blood Orange, and Baby Arugula Salad

SERVES 4

A combination of flavors with the WOW factor!

Vinaigrette

> 1 teaspoon Dijon mustard
>
> 1 teaspoon minced shallot
>
> 1 ounce red wine vinegar
>
> 1 tablespoon honey
>
> Pinch of dried oregano
>
> Salt and freshly ground black pepper
>
> ¼ cup olive oil

Salad

> 1 cup thinly shaved fennel
>
> 4 blood oranges, segmented
>
> 2 avocados, peeled, pitted, and cubed
>
> 8 ounces baby arugula
>
> 4 ounces feta cheese, crumbled

1. Chill four individual salad plates.

2. Add the Dijon, shallot, red wine vinegar, honey, oregano, salt, and pepper to the bowl of a food processor. Blend together well and add the olive oil in a slow steady stream until the vinaigrette is emulsified. If the consistency is too thick, continue blending and add a little warm water to reach the desired consistency.

3. Mix the fennel, oranges, avocado, and arugula in a large bowl and toss with the vinaigrette. Portion the salad equally among the four chilled plates and garnish with the crumbled feta cheese.

✳

Leek, Potato, Wild Mushroom, and Fontina Frittata

SERVES 8

Sunday morning brunch is a perfect time to whip this up!

2 large red potatoes

1 tablespoon unsalted butter

1 tablespoon olive oil

3 leeks, halved lengthwise and thinly sliced

1 cup sliced oyster mushrooms

1 cup sliced cremini mushrooms

1 teaspoon finely chopped fresh thyme

Salt and freshly ground black pepper

1 loaf sourdough bread, cut in ¼-inch slices, crust removed

8 ounces Fontina cheese, shredded

8 large eggs, beaten

1 cup half-and-half

1. Preheat the oven to 350°F.

2. Poke holes in the potatoes with a fork and bake in the oven for 1 hour. Let cool and cut into thin slices. Set aside.

3. Increase the oven temperature to 375°F.

4. In large sauté pan, over medium-high heat, heat the butter and olive oil. Add the leeks, mushrooms, and thyme and sauté until the leeks are translucent. Season with salt and pepper to taste, remove from the heat, and let cool.

5. Spray a 13×9-inch pan with a nonstick cooking spray. Spread the bread slices evenly over the bottom of the baking pan until covered. Sprinkle the cheese evenly over the bread. Layer the leek and mushroom mixture over the cheese and top with the potato slices.

6. In a medium bowl, whisk the eggs and half-and-half. Season the eggs with salt and pepper. Pour the egg mixture over the potatoes and let sit for 5 minutes. Bake in the oven for 1 hour, or until browned and cooked through. Let stand for 10 minutes before cutting and serving.

✳

Grilled Teriyaki Chicken with Pineapple-Mango Salsa

SERVES 4

Pineapple-mango salsa is always a favorite, but serve it with teriyaki and you have a dish to die for!

Teriyaki Chicken

> ½ cup freshly squeezed orange juice
>
> ½ cup low-sodium soy sauce
>
> ½ cup dry sherry
>
> ½ cup canola oil
>
> 1 teaspoon minced fresh garlic
>
> 1 teaspoon minced fresh ginger
>
> ¼ cup firmly packed brown sugar
>
> 4 boneless, skinless chicken breasts

Pineapple-Mango Salsa

> 1 cup fresh pineapple, cut in small dice
>
> 1 cup fresh mango, cut in small dice
>
> ½ cup diced roasted red pepper
>
> ½ cup red onion, cut in small dice
>
> ½ cup chopped fresh cilantro

¼ cup seasoned rice vinegar

¼ cup olive oil

Salt

1. Add the first seven ingredients for chicken marinade in a medium bowl and whisk together. Add the chicken breasts, cover, and marinate in the refrigerator for at least 4 hours or overnight.

2. Mix all ingredients for the salsa in a small bowl. Cover and refrigerate for at least 1 hour prior to serving.

3. Preheat the oven to 300°F. Preheat a grill to medium-high heat. Grill-mark the chicken, about 3 minutes on each side. Transfer the chicken from the grill to a baking dish. Cover with aluminum foil and place in the oven for 15 minutes. Remove from the oven and let rest for 5 minutes. Serve with the salsa.

Radish, Tomato, and Butterleaf Salad with Bay Shrimp and Maytag Blue Cheese

SERVES 4

Crispy veggies and shrimp with tangy blue cheese, what a hit.

Dressing

> ¼ cup sour cream
>
> ¼ cup mayonnaise
>
> ¼ cup buttermilk
>
> 1 tablespoon minced shallot
>
> 1 tablespoon chopped scallion
>
> 1 tablespoon freshly squeezed lemon juice
>
> 4 ounces Bay shrimp
>
> 4 ounces Maytag Blue cheese
>
> Salt and lemon pepper seasoning

Salad

> 1 head butterleaf lettuce, washed and separated into
>   4 portions
>
> 8 radishes, cleaned and sliced
>
> ½ pound green beans, cleaned, trimmed, and blanched
>
> ½ pint baby heirloom tomatoes, washed and stemmed
>
> 2 hard-boiled eggs, peeled and quartered

1. In a small bowl, whisk all the ingredients for the salad dressing together until smooth and creamy. Refrigerate for at least 2 hours or for as long as overnight.

2. Assemble the salad on four serving plates, placing the lettuce in the middle of the plate, the radishes on one side, and the green beans, tomatoes, and egg all on one-quarter of the salad. Spoon the dressing over the lettuce and serve.

✳

Watercress with Beet Carpaccio and Sherry Vinaigrette

SERVES 4

Watercress has just enough spicy bite to hold its own with the pungent beet flavor!

Sherry Vinaigrette

1 tablespoon sherry vinegar

1 teaspoon minced shallots

½ teaspoon Dijon mustard

Salt and freshly ground black pepper

¼ cup olive oil

Carpaccio

>   *4 small golden beets, cooked, cooled, and peeled*
>   *4 small red beets, cooked, cooled, and peeled*
>   *1 bunch hydroponic watercress*
>   *4 ounces goat cheese, crumbled*

1. In a small bowl, whisk together the vinegar, shallots, Dijon, salt, and pepper. Slowly whisk in the olive oil. Refrigerate the vinaigrette until serving time.

2. Chill four salad plates in the freezer. Slice the golden beets very thinly on a mandoline, place in a container, and refrigerate until serving time. Wash the mandoline and slice the red beets very thinly, place in a separate container, and refrigerate until serving time.

3. Just before serving, remove the salad plates from the freezer and alternate golden beets and red beets in a circle in the middle of the plate. Divide the watercress evenly among the plates and place in the middle of the beets. Drizzle the vinaigrette over the watercress and garnish with the crumbled goat cheese.

Watermelon with Shaved Maui Onion and Lime

SERVES 4

This cool refreshing dish makes a great starter, or use as a side with your main course. My clients love the combination of juicy watermelon and sweet Maui onions. I am sure you will, too!

4 cups cubed seedless Pure Heart watermelon

1 cup shaved Maui onion

½ cup mint leaves cut into chiffonade

1 tablespoon freshly squeezed lime juice

1 tablespoon seasoned rice wine vinegar

1 tablespoon sugar

½ teaspoon salt

1 teaspoon peeled and minced fresh ginger

1 teaspoon finely grated lime zest

1. Mix the watermelon, onion, and mint in a medium bowl. Cover with plastic wrap and chill in the refrigerator.

2. Whisk the lime juice, vinegar, sugar, salt, and ginger in a small bowl until well mixed. Just before serving, drizzle the lime mixture over the watermelon mixture and toss lightly. Divide the salad equally among four salad plates and garnish with the lime zest.

Leo

July 23–August 22

MAKE-THE-BEAT-GO-ON FOODS

The Leo food selections are all heart healthy, just what the doctor ordered to keep the Leo tickers thumping along at a nice steady beat. Leos are ambitious, confident, and bighearted with a huge zest for life, which demands the attention of those around them who are readily drawn to the zodiac's resident felines. They will respond in kind and you will find a loyal friend for life.

....

Symbol: Lion
Ruling Planet: Sun
Body Part Ruled: Heart
House Ruled: Fifth, the house of creativity, romance, and children

Element: Fire
Color: Gold
Stone: Ruby
Key Phrase: I will
Trait: Creative
Quality: Fixed

Leo rules the fifth house of creativity, pleasure, and romance with its ruler the sun. Just as all planets revolve around the sun in our solar system, Leos are most content when they are at the center of things with all the attention on them. They shine with all the fire of the sun and dazzle all who come in contact with their brilliance. The symbol for Leo is the regal lion, king of the jungle, and like the lion with his pride, Leos are the kings of their domain, surrounded with their ardent adorers.

They can be considered the social butterfly of the zodiac, get along with people from all walks of life, and are perhaps the ultimate friend, as they are quick to respond should you need their help. Keep your Leo friends' numbers on speed dial, and your next dinner party planning will soon turn into a social event.

LEO IN THE KITCHEN

Lions have a larger-than-life persona, and they regale in the flamboyance associated with the entertainment field. The heart of the lion secretly beats with star quality whether or not he ever takes center stage. Leos love to entertain family, friends, and acquaintances with lavish extravaganzas. They will spare no expense to turn any occasion into the event of the year!

They reign as the stars in their own kitchens. Even those Leos with their handsomely paid personal chefs or full cooking staffs love to make an appearance to see what delectable morsels are being prepared just for them. They pride themselves on being generous both materially and with their words, so will lavish praise on those in the kitchen.

But Leo also loves to take charge of all aspects of the festivities themselves. The Lion is extremely creative and will plan the menu, design the invitations, decorate the dining room, prepare each dish, and be dressed to the nines by the time the first guest arrives. Expect each aspect to be beautiful, unlike anything you have seen before. And while on the subject of beauty, have you checked out the handsome Leo men and the beautiful Leo women? Just look at celebrity chef, Giada De Laurentiis!

Leo does love an audience, so the evening may begin in the kitchen, where your host or hostess will put the finishing touches on a special dish while everyone "oohs and aahs" at the finished product. Or Leo may do steaks with newly created marinade, grilled to order for each of you right before your eyes. And expect it all to be done with flash and flair.

LEO GUESTS

Leos are as adept as invitees as they are as hosts, and will be the shining stars on your guest list. There is a simple rule when including a Leo at your soiree: shine the spotlight on him, and his radiance will light up the room and everyone attending will bask in the illumination.

You should serve sumptuous dishes prepared for a king, exotic, flavorful, dishes anyone would expect to find served at a palace. Be sure to save the head of the table for your Leo guest, where he will be the center of attention. When Leo is truly in his element, he can't help but be gracious, and your other guests won't even realize that the limelight isn't focused on them.

While it could seem like the Leo guest could be high maintenance, this just isn't so. They are courteous, appreciative, and will be quite enthusiastic in thanking you. When the Lion is fully sated, you will have him purring contently in no time at all.

A table set with fine golden linens and a centerpiece in shades of burgundy and gold will present a wonderful ambiance which the Lion will appreciate. Goblets of ruby crystal filled with luscious wine will be perfect for Leo. Beautifully lit candles are always lovely on any dining table, but with a Leo in the room the candlelight may pale in comparison.

FEATURED LEO MAKE-THE-BEAT-GO-ON FOODS

All these foods are great for Leo and the heart, but all signs will benefit from the heart-protecting properties.

Ahi. Canned tuna is okay, but it just can't compare to the fresh. Ahi is a great source of protein, selenium, omega-3s, phosphorus, potassium, and vitamins B_1, B_3, and B_6, all of which contribute to cardiovascular health. It is also very high in tryptophan, the essential amino acid that can make you feel sleepy, making ahi an excellent choice to provide a little relaxation for the hearts of very active Leos.

Almonds. These nutritional nuts are real powerhouses packed with fiber, plant omega-3s, calcium, folic acid, phytosterols, vitamin E, magnesium, and potassium that are all great for the heart. Flavonoids in the skins help lower LDL cholesterol and the risk of heart disease. These ancient nuts were one of the first cultivated crops, have been of benefit for thousands of years, and were especially eaten by royalty, making almonds just what the king of the jungle needs.

Black Beans. High in molybdenum, an essential mineral for the body, B complex vitamins, folate, magnesium, protein, and soluble fiber, these legumes aid in the prevention of free radical injury to the heart and can lower heart-attack risk. Adding black beans to soups and salads will aid cardiovascular upkeep for Leos and other signs with any heart concerns.

Lobster. Lobster is the perfect exotic shellfish for Leo who prizes the very best life has to offer them. No entrée draws attention like a beautiful red lobster served in all its glory! And no one can appreciate it quite like the flamboyant Leo! But lobster is also heart healthy, which may be surprising. It is low in fat and cholesterol, high in protein, and loaded with phosphorus, selenium, zinc, vitamin B_{12}, and omega-3 fatty acid, which protects against heart disease. So anyone who *loves* lobster should take their lead from the Lion.

Opakapaka. Everyone has heard of, and more than likely eaten, red snapper, but you haven't lived until you have eaten opakapaka, Hawaiian pink snapper! Leos know how to live large and should order opakapaka from their local fishmonger when they can't make it to the islands for a spectacular sunset dinner. This snapper is high in ultralean protein, vitamins B_6 and B_{12}, selenium, and phosphorus, and low in fat. In addition it is laden with omegas and has anti-inflammatory properties. It is a star in the fish department, making it a natural for Leos who visualize themselves as the shining stars of the zodiac. And rightly so, as nothing beams brighter than Leo's symbol, the sun!

Papaya. This tropical fruit is packed with vitamins A, C, E, and K, all antioxidants that benefit the cardiovascular system and prevent atherosclerosis. Papaya also contains carpain, another benefit for the heart. Some feel papaya has the power of rejuvenation, which can contribute to keeping the heart of the Lion young and healthy.

Saffron. These fragile threads are highly coveted as the most costly and exceptional spice in the world, making it number one for Leos. They adore anything that elicits star power and feel they are all-deserving of the best the world has to offer. And it is good for them. High in omega-3 and -6 fatty acids, saffron can relieve high blood pressure and high cholesterol. It is rich in manganese, folate, copper, and potassium, all heart healthy. These technical terms simply mean the Leo heart will be kept beating in rhythm for years to come. All other signs concerned about the pitter-pat of their own hearts should head to the nearest spice store.

Tomatoes. Extremely high in vitamin C and a good source for vitamins A and K. Tomatoes are also loaded with lycopene, an antioxidant that prevents heart disease. All signs should join Leos in feasting on these heart-healthy treats a few times a week, especially during tomato season, which just happens to hit its peak when the sun is in Leo.

✳

Ahi Tartare on Wonton with Wasabi Crème Fraîche and Tobiko

SERVES 8

This is one of my favorite appetizers and a real showstopper, and Leo is all about show!

Tartare

1 pound best-quality, sushi-grade ahi tuna, cut in very
 small dice

¼ cup Maui onion or other sweet onion, cut in small dice

2 scallions, finely chopped

½ teaspoon minced fresh garlic

½ teaspoon minced fresh ginger

1 teaspoon black sesame seeds

1 teaspoon white sesame seeds

¼ cup low-sodium soy sauce

2 tablespoons seasoned rice vinegar

1 tablespoon sesame oil

1 tablespoon olive oil

Pinch of brown sugar

Wasabi Crème Fraîche

　　2 tablespoons wasabi powder

　　2 tablespoons water

　　½ cup sour cream

　　¼ cup heavy cream

　　2 cups canola oil

　　One 16-ounce package wonton wrappers

　　4 ounces tobiko

1. In a medium bowl, mix together the tuna, onions, garlic, ginger, and sesame seeds. Set aside. In a small bowl, whisk together the soy sauce, vinegar, sesame oil, and brown sugar. Pour over the tuna mixture and mix to combine. Cover with plastic wrap and refrigerate.

2. In a small bowl, stir the wasabi and water together to make a paste. Mix the sour cream and heavy cream into the wasabi mixture until thoroughly blended. Pour into a squirt bottle and refrigerate.

3. Heat the canola oil in a wok over medium-high heat for 5 minutes, or until the oil is hot. Line a baking sheet with paper towels and set aside. Test the oil with one wonton to see if it is hot enough; the wonton should pop right to the surface and turn golden brown. Use tongs to remove the wonton wrapper from the oil and place it on the lined sheet. Continue until all of the wontons are cooked.

4. Arrange the cooked wontons on a serving platter. Using a 1-ounce ice cream scoop, place the tuna mixture on top of the wontons. Shake the squirt bottle well and squeeze the crème fraîche in a zig-zag pattern over the wonton. Garnish with the tobiko, and serve.

✳

Almond Pound Cake with Caramelized Pears and Mascarpone

SERVES 8

I first created this for one of my favorite clients and it has become a favorite on my menu.

Cake

> 2 ½ cups all-purpose flour
>
> ½ teaspoon baking soda
>
> ½ teaspoon salt
>
> 2 cups granulated sugar
>
> 16 tablespoons (2 sticks) unsalted butter, softened at
>   room temperature
>
> 5 large eggs
>
> ½ cup buttermilk
>
> 2 teaspoons almond extract
>
> 1 cup sliced almonds

Glaze

　　8 tablespoons (1 stick) unsalted butter, melted

　　2 cups confectioners' sugar

　　1 teaspoon almond extract

　　2 tablespoons warm water

　　½ cup mascarpone cheese, softened

　　1 vanilla bean, split lengthwise, seeds scraped

Pears

　　2 tablespoons (¼ stick) unsalted butter

　　½ cup firmly packed light brown sugar

　　6 red Bartlett pears, peeled and sliced

1. Preheat the oven to 350°F.

2. In a small bowl, sift together the flour, baking soda, and salt and set aside. In a large mixing bowl, cream the butter and sugar together on medium-high speed with an electric mixer until light and fluffy. Add the eggs one at a time on medium speed, mixing thoroughly. Add the buttermilk and almond extract and continue beating. Scrape down the sides of the bowl and add the flour mixture on low speed.

3. Divide the batter between two 9×5-inch greased loaf pans and sprinkle the top with sliced almonds. Bake for 40 to 45 minutes until golden brown and baked through. Test with a skewer; if it comes out clean when inserted in the center the cake is done. Let cool for 15 minutes, then turn out onto a wire rack. Continue cooling for 15 minutes.

4. In a small mixing bowl, mix the mascarpone cheese and vanilla bean seeds on medium speed until light and fluffy. Set aside.

5. In a medium mixing bowl, mix the butter and confectioners' sugar on low speed. Add the almond extract and water and continue beating until smooth. Poke holes in the top of the cake with a skewer. Drizzle the glaze over the top of the cake evenly. Let rest for 30 minutes before serving.

6. Melt the butter in small saucepan. Add the brown sugar and stir constantly. Stir in the pears and simmer over low heat for 5 minutes, stirring constantly. Remove from the heat and serve over a slice of cake with a dollop of mascarpone cheese.

Creamy Polenta with Black Bean Ragout

SERVES 8

The black beans and polenta are such a great team!

Black Beans

    1 teaspoon coriander seeds, toasted

    2 teaspoons cumin seeds, toasted

    1 tablespoon dried oregano leaves, toasted

    1 tablespoon olive oil

    1 tablespoon unsalted butter

    1 yellow onion, cut into medium dice

    3 garlic cloves, minced

    1 red bell pepper, seeded, membranes removed, and cut
        into medium dice

    1 pound dried black beans, cooked according to package
        directions

    2 cups ripe yellow and red tomatoes, diced

    ½ cup chopped fresh cilantro

    Salt

Polenta

    1 tablespoon olive oil

    1 tablespoon unsalted butter plus 4 tablespoons (½ stick),
        cut into small pieces

    ½ cup minced yellow onion

1 teaspoon minced garlic

1 tablespoon chopped fresh oregano

1 quart organic chicken broth

1 teaspoon salt

1 cup dry polenta

½ cup heavy cream

1 cup Monterey Jack cheese

½ cup chopped fresh mint

4 ounces goat cheese, crumbled

1. In an electric grinder, grind together the toasted coriander, cumin seed, and dried oregano. Set aside. In a large pot, heat the olive oil and butter over medium-high heat. Add the onions, garlic, and bell pepper and cook until the onions are translucent, about 3 minutes. Stir the ground spices into the vegetable mixture. Add the black beans and keep stirring. Bring to simmer and let cook for 20 minutes. Add the tomatoes and cilantro and cook for another 10 minutes. Set aside.

2. To make the polenta, heat the olive oil and the 1 tablespoon of butter in a large heavy-bottomed pot over medium-high heat. Add the onions, garlic, and oregano and cook until the onions are translucent. Add the chicken broth and salt and bring to a boil. Gradually add the polenta in a slow, steady stream, stirring constantly for 5 minutes to avoid lumps. Add the 4 tablespoons of butter pieces to the polenta, reduce the heat, and simmer for 10 minutes. Add the cream and cheese and stir until the cheese is melted.

3. Pour the polenta into a shallow serving bowl, make a hole in the center, and spoon in the black beans. Garnish with the crumbled goat cheese and chopped mint and serve.

Lobster Macaroni and Cheese

SERVES 8

My Leo client was getting married and asked me if I could make this for his bride.

8 tablespoons (1 stick) unsalted butter, cut into pieces

½ cup all-purpose flour

1 quart half-and-half

2 teaspoons salt

½ teaspoon freshly grated nutmeg

¼ teaspoon white pepper

3 cups shredded sharp, white cheddar cheese

2 cups shredded Fontina cheese

2 pounds cooked lobster meat

1 pound penne pasta, cooked and drained

1 cup panko bread crumbs

1 cup grated Parmigiano-Reggiano

¼ cup melted butter

1. Preheat the oven to 350°F.

2. Melt the stick of butter in a heavy-bottomed pot over medium heat. Using a whisk and stirring constantly, add the flour to the butter and continue stirring for 2 minutes until the roux is bubbling. Gradually add the milk, stirring constantly, and cook until thickened and smooth. Add the salt, nutmeg, and pepper. Remove the pot from the heat and whisk in the cheddar and Fontina cheeses until the cheeses are melted and incorporated into the sauce. Stir in the lobster meat and pasta and mix thoroughly.

3. Spray eight 10-ounce ramekins with nonstick cooking spray. Fill the ramekins equally with the macaroni and cheese, leaving room for the bread crumb topping. Mix the panko and Parmigiano-Reggiano together in a small bowl. Add the melted butter and mix together until crumbly. Top each ramekin with the bread crumb mixture and bake in the oven for 30 minutes, or until nicely browned and bubbly.

Crab-Stuffed Opakapaka with Lobster Bordelaise

SERVES 4

Opakapaka is the best fish on the planet! In my opinion.

Opakapaka

Four 5-ounce pieces opakapaka (Hawaiian pink snapper)

4 ounces fresh crabmeat

1 cup all-purpose flour

1 teaspoon salt

1 teaspoon paprika

3 eggs

2 cups panko bread crumbs

1 cup canola oil

Lobster Bordelaise

3 tablespoons unsalted butter

1 tablespoon olive oil

1 shallot, minced

1 cup carrots, cut into small dice

2 tablespoons flour

1 teaspoon lobster paste

¼ cup dry sherry

1 cup heavy cream

3 sprigs fresh thyme

1 cup finely chopped cooked lobster meat
1 tablespoon chopped fresh parsley

1. Preheat the oven to 300°F.

2. Cut a slit in the side of each of the opakapaka pieces and stuff with the crabmeat. Close the opening and set the fish aside.

3. Mix the flour, salt, and paprika in a ziplock bag and shake together well. Pour the seasoned flour into a pan or shallow dish. Beat the eggs in a separate pan or dish. Put the panko in a third pan or dish. Dredge the fish in the flour, dip in the egg mixture, and coat with the panko bread crumbs. Heat the oil in a large sauté pan over medium-high heat. Add the fish and sauté on each side for 2 to 3 minutes until golden brown. Transfer to a baking dish and bake in the oven, uncovered, for 20 minutes.

4. Meanwhile, prepare the lobster bordelaise. In a large saucepan, heat 1 tablespoon of the butter and the olive oil over medium-high heat. Add the shallots and carrots and sauté for 3 minutes. Reduce the heat to medium and add the remaining 2 tablespoons of butter and the flour to the pan, stirring constantly. Stir in the lobster paste and dry sherry. Add the cream and thyme sprigs and continue stirring until the sauce starts to thicken. Reduce the heat and simmer for 5 minutes. Remove the thyme sprigs, add the lobster meat, and combine with the sauce.

5. Serve the fish with the sauce and pieces of lobster ladled over the top. Garnish with chopped parsley.

✳

Seared Scallops with Saffron Butter

Saffron is the most expensive spice in the world! Perfect for the Leo!

Saffron Butter Sauce

> 8 tablespoons (1 stick) unsalted butter, cut in small pieces
>> and frozen, plus 1 tablespoon
> 1 tablespoon olive oil
> ¼ cup minced shallots
> ¼ cup freshly squeezed lemon juice
> ¼ cup white wine
> ¼ teaspoon saffron
> 2 tablespoons all-purpose flour
> 1 cup heavy cream

Scallops

> 1 pound sea scallops
> Salt and freshly ground black pepper
> 1 tablespoon olive oil
> 1 tablespoon unsalted butter

2 plum tomatoes, cut into very small dice

¼ cup chopped flat-leaf parsley

Cooked rice for serving

1. Put the cut butter pieces in the freezer.

2. In a large sauté pan, heat the oil and the remaining table-spoon of butter over medium-high heat. Add the shallots and sauté until translucent. Add the lemon juice, white wine, and saffron, reduce the heat to low, and let simmer for 5 minutes. Add the frozen butter pieces and flour to the pan and whisk until the sauce has thickened. Whisk the heavy cream into the sauce and simmer.

3. Clean the scallops and remove the muscle from the side. Season the scallops with salt and pepper to taste and set aside. In heavy-bottomed sauté pan, heat the olive oil and butter over high heat. When the oil is hot, add the scallops and sear on each side for 2 to 3 minutes, or until golden brown. If all the scallops will not fit in the pan, cook them in small batches and transfer the cooked scallops to a plate, and cover them with foil.

4. Serve the scallops over rice, drizzled with the saffron sauce. Garnish with the diced tomato and chopped parsley.

*

Papaya Stuffed with Shrimp Ceviche

SERVES 2

This is so wonderful on a hot summer day with a glass of white!

> 1 tablespoon kosher salt
> ½ pound small raw shrimp, peeled and deveined
> Juice of 1 lime plus ½ lime, cut into wedges
> 1 teaspoon lime zest
> ½ cup coconut milk
> ½ teaspoon minced fresh ginger
> ½ Maui onion, cut into small dice
> 2 tablespoons cilantro, chopped
> 1 tomato, seeded and cut into small dice
> Sea salt
> 1 ripe papaya, peeled, seeded, and cubed, plus 1 extra
>   papaya, cut lengthwise and seeded

1. Bring a medium pot of water to a boil and add salt. Add shrimp to the boiling water for 1 minute, then transfer immediately to an ice bath. Drain shrimp thoroughly and set aside. Mix lime juice, lime zest, coconut milk, ginger, onion, 1 tablespoon of cilantro, and tomato in a medium glass bowl. Stir in the shrimp. Cover the shrimp and refrigerate for 30 minutes. Remove from refrigerator, add cubed papaya, season with salt, and mix together.

2. Fill each half of papaya with ceviche and garnish with lime wedges and the remaining tablespoon of cilantro.

*

Heirloom Tomato and Bufala di Mozzarella Napoleon
SERVES 4

Growing up in a prime farm area, I am completely spoiled when it comes to the king of the crop with tomatoes. If you can't get good tomatoes, don't make this salad. It all starts with the tomato!

4 large slices rustic country-style bread, brushed with olive
oil on both sides

4 large salad plates, chilled

4 heirloom tomatoes, approximately the same size in four
different colors (orange, red, yellow, and green), cut
into 4 slices each

Two 8-ounce balls bufala di mozzarella, cut into 16 slices

20 large fresh basil leaves, 16 whole for stacking and
4 rolled and cut into chiffonade for garnish

Sea salt and fresh ground black pepper

Villa Manodori balsamic vinegar

Extra-virgin olive oil

1. Heat a grill over medium heat. Grill the bread on both sides so it is marked. Set aside.

2. Assemble two napoleons on each plate by stacking one slice of the mozzarella with a basil leaf, and one slice of tomato, then repeat. There should be two slices of mozzarella, two slices of tomato, and two pieces of basil. Season with salt and pepper to taste. Drizzle with vinegar and oil. Garnish with the chiffonade of basil.

3. Cut the grilled bread in half on the diagonal and serve on a plate with the napoleons.

Virgo

August 23–September 22

NERVE-SETTLING FOODS

All these foods have been carefully selected for Virgo, as this sign rules the nervous system. These foods will keep Virgos balanced and on an even keel, able to digest, rest, and handle all that stress that occurs when they are trying to be perfect. All other signs that need to be on top of their "fight or flight" responses can certainly benefit from these foods.

Symbol: The Virgin
Ruling Planet: Mercury
Body Part Ruled: Nervous system
House Ruled: Sixth, the house of health and service

Element: Earth
Color: Navy blue
Stone: Sapphire
Key Phrase: I analyze
Trait: Conscientiousness
Quality: Mutable

Virgo rules the sixth house of duty, health, and service, along with the ruling planet Mercury. Those individuals born under the sign of Virgo are the zodiac's critics and natural analysts. They have a quick wit, are master communicators, and deep thinkers. But above all else, it's their keen powers of observation that are most notable; nothing gets past them. They have the eyes of a hawk ready to swoop down on its prey.

These diligent hard workers can ferret out any issues related to cash flow of even the most high-profile corporation. They are perfectionists who will stay the course until every ledger column has been tallied, checked, rechecked, every *i* dotted, *t* crossed, and the annual report bound, ready for delivery. But they *must* take care of their health at the same time and be mindful of that overstressed nervous system!

VIRGO IN THE KITCHEN

The Virgo natives feel quite at home in the kitchen, as they truly love even the most elaborate and perplexing equipment and gadgets. Nothing pleases them more than scrutinizing the directions, and figuring out the perfect way to slice and dice to create a delicious meal.

Virgos make the perfect hosts or hostesses as they plan everything down to the very last detail. If you are one of the fortunate who makes it onto their guest list, the evening will far surpass any expectations you could possibly have. The menu will be devised with all the planning given for heads of state or visiting dignitaries. Since they are health conscious, the Virgo chef will give careful consideration to any food restrictions for their guests, but don't think for one minute that the meal will be boring or tasteless. You will never realize there have been any "substitutions" in the recipe.

Virgos are perfectionists in everything they do, so how they move in the kitchen is no different than any other endeavor they undertake. They have such attention to detail they are probably better than any other sign when it comes to replicating the most complicated recipes. Virgo natives can analyze the complex ingredients and directions of the most prestigious French cookbook, convert the recipe to a healthier version, follow all the steps to a tee, and produce a delicious meal that will have you longing for a stroll along the Seine.

VIRGO GUESTS

Virgos adore an invitation to dine as your guest at any party, as long as it is cultured and classy. Their symbol, the Virgin, might suggest that they could be prudes and shy away from the tawdry or unrefined, but don't be mistaken. It is just that they much prefer this type of social engagement rather than the casual night about town where they may not connect on an intellectual level. Virgos look forward to brilliant exchanges with other like-minded guests, stimulating conversations, and witty banter.

They are sophisticated, polished additions to your most refined dinner. Virgos' dream seating arrangement would be between the self-sacrificing Gandhi and the Mayo Clinic medical director, satisfying both their connection to duty and service and their thirst for health concerns. With this not being possible, seat them between two other analytical wizards and they will be thrilled.

Set an elegant table with navy linens with silver accents— Mercury's color. Silver candlesticks with shimmering silver candles will certainly set the tone. For a special touch, add individual flower arrangements of asters in little silver vases with tendrils of ivy strewn down the center of the table. This extra attention to detail will definitely delight any Virgo and set the mood for the most exquisite event of the season.

FEATURED VIRGO NERVE-SETTLING FOODS

All these foods are great for Virgo and the nervous system, but all signs will benefit from the nerve-settling properties.

Bok Choy. This Chinese green is protective against depression and very important for nerve functioning. It also protects the nervous system, making it excellent for Virgos who need to keep those nerves in check. Bok choy is high in vitamins A, C, and K, potassium, and calcium. Potassium and calcium are both crucial for muscle and nerve relaxation, so maybe Virgo natives should indulge in a bedtime bowl of steamed bok choy instead of that glass of milk.

Broccolini. High in vitamins A, C, and K, broccolini helps with vitamin D metabolism, which can keep the Virgo nervous system depression free. The Virgo power lunch should include some nice steamed or sautéed broccolini to work as an antidepressant. Or better yet, they could schedule dinner reservations at the best Chinese restaurant in town where they can feast on broccolini and beef with a side of bok choy and have their ultimate relaxing meal. Of course they may need a designated driver or take a cab home as they could just be on tranquil overload!

Grass-fed Beef. Very high in tryptophan, which makes you sleepy, lean organic beef is just what those highly analytical Virgos need to rest their overactive minds and get a good night's rest. This is definitely a meal Virgos should have in the evening as they just might not make it back to their high-stress jobs after lunch if they are too relaxed! Any other sign needing a peaceful night should make a lean organic steak their Ambien substitute.

Lavender. This fragrant herb should surround all Virgos, in their gardens, medicine cabinets, and in their pantries. It is of great benefit to the nervous system, easing stress headaches and depression, facilitating relaxation, and the overall communication among all nerves in the body. It's not unusual that lavender would be the Virgo herb, since "communication" is of such importance to Virgo and the sign rules the nervous system. A fragrant lavender eye pillow would be great help for a Virgo's good night's sleep to keep them alert for their daily on-the-job perfection everyone expects.

Lentils. Lentil soup, especially Indian *kitchari,* is soothing and good for the nervous system. Lentils are a good source of protein, calcium, folate, and other minerals and vitamins. These minerals help in maintaining energy and keeping the nervous system strong and vital. The lack of folate in the system can cause depression, which will send the analytical

Virgo into a tizzy, something so against their nature. Virgos should take a much-needed break and head to the closest Indian restaurant once a week to recharge on their fill of these feel-good legumes.

Pumpkin. While Virgos definitely know about "fight or flight," they also have "relax and renew" capabilities that come from the calmer version of themselves or the parasympathetic nervous system. Pumpkin is loaded with vitamins and minerals that help manage stress and make it easier for Virgos to unwind and their nervous systems to rest. Sounds like pumpkin pie is just what the doctor ordered for these slightly intense people!

Split Peas. These great dried peas have been used as healing remedies as well as a great protein source for hundreds of years. They are nutritious and delicious with antidepressant, anti-anxiety properties, great for the Virgo nervous system. Other health properties also include fiber, tryptophan, manganese, and folate, all of which will stimulate the touchy nervous systems of those who are prone to depression, which plagues the overworked Virgo. A nice bowl of split pea soup will really soothe those frazzled nerves!

Turkey. Turkey is the ultimate in tryptophan content, as well as ample levels of vitamin B_3 and B_6, selenium, zinc, and iron. Not only does it rank high in mood-enhancing properties, but turkey also promotes sleep, which will relieve both stress and depression when those Virgo powerhouses crash and burn from overworking their finely tuned nervous systems. With a little sleep and a little relaxation, they will be right back on top of the analytical game in no time. All other signs should follow their Virgo friends down the turkey aisle of the corner market!

*

Braised Baby Bok Choy with Red Peppers and Oyster Mushrooms
SERVES 4

The oyster mushrooms really make this dish!

4 cups chicken broth (1 cup for bok choy & 3 cups for rice)

2 tablespoons (¼ stick) unsalted butter

½ teaspoon salt

One 15-ounce bag Jade Pearl rice

1 tablespoon olive oil

1 tablespoon sesame oil

1 teaspoon minced fresh ginger

1 teaspoon minced fresh garlic

½ pound oyster mushrooms

12 heads baby bok choy

2 roasted red bell peppers, seeded, peeled, and cut into
   strips
2 tablespoons store-bought black bean garlic sauce
2 tablespoons dry sherry
1 tablespoon honey
2 tablespoons toasted sesame seeds

1. In a medium saucepan, heat 3 cups of the chicken broth, the butter, and salt over medium-high heat and bring to a boil. Add the rice, reduce the heat to a simmer, cover, and cook for 20 minutes, or until the liquid is absorbed. Remove from the heat.

2. In a wok, heat the olive and sesame oils over medium-high heat. When the oil is hot, add the ginger, garlic, and oyster mushrooms and stir constantly for 2 to 3 minutes. Add the bok choy and continue stirring for 5 minutes. Add the bell pepper strips, chicken broth, black bean sauce, sherry, and honey, reduce the heat, and simmer for 5 minutes.

3. Fluff the rice with a fork. Place a scoop of rice in each of four shallow bowls. Spoon the braised bok choy over the top. Garnish with the toasted sesame seeds.

✳

Orecchiette Pasta with Broccolini and Pecorino
SERVES 8

This is such a light and wonderful pasta!

> 1 pound orecchiette pasta
>
> 1 pound broccolini, trimmed and cut in bite-sized pieces
>
> 2 tablespoons olive oil
>
> 4 tablespoons (½ stick) unsalted butter
>
> 1 tablespoon minced garlic
>
> Salt and freshly ground black pepper
>
> 1 cup grated pecorino Romano cheese

1. Bring two large pots of salted water to a boil over high heat. Add the pasta to one pot and cook for 9 to 11 minutes, or until al dente. Add the broccolini to the other pot of boiling water and blanche for 5 minutes. Drain the broccolini in a colander and transfer to an ice bath. Drain and set aside.

2. In a large skillet, heat the olive oil and butter over medium-high heat. Add the garlic and broccolini and sauté for 3 minutes. Season with salt and pepper to taste. Drain the pasta and transfer it to a large serving bowl. Pour the broccolini over the pasta and toss together to combine. Sprinkle with the grated cheese.

✳

Grilled New York Strips with Portobello Mushrooms and Horseradish Sauce

SERVES 2

Every now and then I need a good grilled steak with the works! This is that steak!

Marinade

1 tablespoon steak seasoning of choice

1 tablespoon stone-ground mustard

1 tablespoon minced fresh garlic

¼ cup Worcestershire Sauce

¼ cup olive oil

2 New York strip steaks

Horseradish Sauce

½ cup sour cream

½ cup mayonnaise

½ cup horseradish

Mushrooms

> 1 tablespoon olive oil
>
> 1 teaspoon minced fresh garlic
>
> 1 large yellow onion, halved lengthwise and sliced into
>   half-moons
>
> 1 portobello mushroom, stemmed and thinly sliced
>
> Salt and freshly ground black pepper

1. In a small bowl, mix all the ingredients for the marinade. Place the steaks in a shallow container, and cover with the marinade. Cover the container and refrigerate overnight.

2. In a small bowl, mix together the sour cream, mayonnaise, and horseradish. Cover and refrigerate for 1 hour.

3. In a large sauté pan, heat the olive oil over medium-high heat. Add the garlic and onions and sauté until the onions are translucent. Add the mushrooms and sauté another 5 minutes, or until the mushrooms are tender. Season with salt and pepper to taste.

4. Preheat a grill to medium-high heat. Grill the steaks on both sides to the desired internal temperature (120–130°F for rare, 130–140°F for medium rare, 135–145°F for medium, 145–155°F for medium well, 155°F and over for well done). Remove steaks to a plate and rest them for 10 minutes. Cut into strips on the diagonal and serve with the mushrooms and onions and horseradish sauce.

✳

French Green Lentils and Roasted Vegetable Stew

SERVES 8

I love lentils, and roasting the vegetables first really enhances this dish!

2 yellow onions, cut into medium dice

3 carrots, peeled and cut into medium dice

4 celery stalks, cut into medium dice

½ pound cremini mushrooms, washed and quartered

1 pound plum tomatoes, washed and quartered

5 tablespoons olive oil

1 teaspoon sea salt

1 tablespoon unsalted butter

2 cloves garlic, minced

6 cups organic chicken stock

1 bay leaf

6 sprigs fresh thyme

2 cups French green lentils

2 teaspoons ground cumin

Salt and freshly ground black pepper

1 cup sour cream

½ cup chopped flat-leaf parsley

1. Preheat the oven to 400°F. Toss the onions, carrots, celery, mushrooms, and tomatoes with 4 tablespoons of the olive oil and salt. Spread out the vegetables on a baking sheet and roast in the oven for 45 minutes, or until the vegetables are starting to brown.

2. In a large heavy-bottomed pot, heat the remaining tablespoons of olive oil and the butter over medium-high heat. Add the garlic and sauté for 2 minutes. Add 4 cups of the chicken stock and bring to a boil. Add the bay leaf, thyme, and lentils, reduce the heat, cover, and simmer for 30 to 35 minutes until the lentils are tender. Add the roasted vegetables, the remaining 2 cups of the chicken stock, and the cumin to the lentils and continue to simmer for 20 minutes. Remove the bay leaf and thyme sprigs before serving. Serve with a dollop of sour cream and garnish with chopped parsley.

＊

Frosted Lavender and Lemon Zest Shortbread Cookies

MAKES 3 DOZEN COOKIES

I live across the gulch from the most beautiful lavender farm. If you are ever on Maui, make sure to visit Alii Lavender Farm or visit them online: www.aliikulalavender.com.

Cookies

> 3 cups all-purpose flour
>
> ½ pound (2 sticks) unsalted butter
>
> ¾ cup confectioners' sugar
>
> 1 teaspoon unsprayed, dried lavender buds, crushed
>
> ¼ teaspoon lemon zest

Icing

> 2 cups confectioners' sugar
>
> 1 tablespoon water
>
> 1 tablespoon butter
>
> 1 tablespoon light corn syrup
>
> ½ teaspoon finely grated lemon zest

1. Measure the flour into a bowl and set aside.

2. Cream the butter and sugar in the bowl of an electric mixer on medium speed. Add the lavender buds and lemon zest and mix until blended. Add small amounts of the sifted flour, a little at a time, and mix until fully incorporated.

3. Shape the dough into a log and wrap in plastic wrap. Continue shaping the log into a long rectangle with even sides. Chill in the freezer for 2 hours.

4. Preheat the oven to 325°F.

5. Slice the chilled dough into ½-inch-thick cookies, and place on cookie sheets. Bake for 20 minutes, or until lightly golden. Remove from the oven and transfer to a rack to cool.

6. In the bowl of an electric mixer, beat all the icing ingredients, except the lemon zest, at medium speed until smoth, adding additional water if necessary. And lemon zest and mix to incorporate. Brush over cookies.

Pumpkin Spice Cupcakes with Cream Cheese Frosting and Crystallized Ginger

MAKES 24 CUPCAKES

Crystallized ginger really enhances the flavor of pumpkin.

Cupcakes

    2 cups all-purpose flour
    1 cup granulated sugar
    1 cup firmly packed brown sugar
    ½ teaspoon salt
    1 teaspoon baking soda
    1 teaspoon baking powder
    2 teaspoons ground cinnamon
    ½ teaspoon freshly grated nutmeg
    Pinch of ground cloves
    3 large eggs
    1 cup vegetable oil
    2 cups fresh mashed cooked pumpkin

2 teaspoons vanilla extract

1 cup chopped walnuts or pecans

Frosting

3 ½ cups confectioners' sugar

One 8-ounce package cream cheese

8 tablespoons (1 stick) unsalted butter, softened

1 ¼ teaspoons vanilla extract

1 cup crystallized ginger, chopped fine

1. Preheat the oven to 350°F.

2. In a medium bowl, combine all the sifted dry ingredients. Set aside.

3. In the bowl of an electric mixer, beat the eggs, oil, pumpkin, and vanilla on medium for 3 minutes. Gradually stir the dry ingredients into the pumpkin mixture until completely blended. Stir in 1 cup of the toasted walnuts.

4. Line two standard muffin pans with paper liners. Divide the batter evenly among the 24 wells. Bake the cupcakes for 20 to 25 minutes until a toothpick inserted in the center comes out clean. Allow to cool in pan.

5. In a medium bowl, combine the confectioners' sugar, cream cheese, butter, and vanilla. Beat until smooth. Frost the cooled cupcakes and garnish with crystallized ginger.

✳

Split Pea Soup with Roasted Pork Belly

SERVES 8

I started using pork belly with this because of my husband. It reminds him of his European roots.

12 thick slices pork belly

1 onion, cut into small dice

2 carrots, peeled and cut into small dice

3 celery stalks, cut into small dice

3 garlic cloves, minced

6 cups chicken stock

1 pound split peas, rinsed and drained

1 bay leaf

6 sprigs fresh thyme

Salt and freshly ground black pepper

½ cup chopped flat-leaf parsley

1. Heat a large heavy-bottomed pot over medium heat. Add the pork belly and cook until crisp. Transfer to paper towels to absorb excess fat. Leave just enough of the fat from the pork belly in the pot to brown the vegetables.

2. Add the onions, carrot, celery, and garlic to the fat in the pot and sauté until the onion is translucent. Add the water, split peas, bay leaf, and thyme.

3. Crumble 8 pieces of the pork belly and add to the soup. Bring to a boil, reduce the heat, and simmer for 1½ hours, stirring occasionally, or until the peas are soft. Season to taste with salt and pepper. Remove and discard the bay leaf. Ladle the soup into bowls and garnish with chopped parsley and the remaining crumbled pork belly pieces.

Lemon Thyme–Roasted Turkey Breast with Butternut Squash

SERVES 4

I made this for Jenny McCarthy while we were in Jacksonville, Florida, for a month. Needless to say, I have made it for her many times since.

Marinade

> 2 tablespoons minced garlic
>
> 1 tablespoon chopped fresh lemon thyme, plus 10 sprigs
>
> 1 tablespoon chopped fresh sage
>
> Juice of 2 lemons
>
> 6 tablespoons olive oil

Turkey

> One 5- to 6-pound bone-in turkey breast
>
> Salt and freshly ground black pepper
>
> 1 butternut squash, peeled, seeded, and cut into small
>   chunks
>
> 1 tablespoon finely chopped fresh rosemary leaves

1. Mix the garlic, chopped lemon thyme, sage, lemon juice, and 4 tablespoons of the olive oil in a small bowl and whisk together. Set the marinade aside.

2. Season the turkey breast with salt and pepper. Spray a shallow glass baking dish with nonstick spray and lay the turkey breast in the dish, skin side up. Gently loosen the skin from the breast of turkey and pour the marinade over, being sure to get some of the marinade between the skin and breast meat. Lay the remaining thyme sprigs on top of the turkey breast, cover, and refrigerate for 2 hours.

3. Preheat the oven to 350°F. Remove the turkey breast from the refrigerator and place into the oven. Roast for 1½ to 2 hours, basting every 20 minutes.

4. When the turkey breast has roasted for 45 minutes, toss the butternut squash with the chopped rosemary, the remaining 2 tablespoons of olive oil, and salt and pepper. Spread it out evenly over a baking sheet and place on rack in the oven. Roast the squash for remaining cooking time for the turkey, 45 minutes or until browned and tender.

5. Toward the end of the cooking, check the turkey and if the skin is getting too brown, cover it loosely with aluminum foil. At the end of the cooking time, check the internal temperature of the turkey; it should read 170°F. Remove the turkey breast from the oven, along with the butternut squash, cover, and let rest for 15 minutes. Slice the turkey and ladle the pan juices over the meat. Serve with the butternut squash.

Libra

September 23–October 22

WASH-AWAY-THAT-WASTE FOODS

All these foods have been carefully selected for Libra, as this sign rules the kidneys. These foods are just what the doctor ordered to keep Librans free from toxins and well-balanced. The scales, their symbol, represent how off-kilter Libras can be when things are not in perfect alignment, which keeps them from being their charming adorable selves. So they and all other signs in need of a good "flushing" can certainly benefit from these foods.

....

Symbol: The Scales
Ruling Planet: Venus
Body Part Ruled: Kidneys
House Ruled: Seventh, the house
   of partnerships
Element: Air

Colors: Blue, pink
Stone: Opal
Key Phrase: I balance
Trait: Charm
Quality: Cardinal

Libra rules the seventh house of partnerships and relationships, which reign supreme in the eyes of any Libran, along with its ruler Venus. They are the ones always seeking equilibrium in their lives and in the lives of those around them. They cherish balance and abhor any discord.

Peace and harmony could be the motto for Librans. They seem to be the perpetual "fence sitters" of the zodiac, never making up their minds about anything or taking a stand. But this just isn't true. The intellectual Libra would rather be perceived as an "airhead" than offend others, often telling people what they want to hear for fear of any confrontation. Fundamentally they are quintessentially adept at pleasing others.

LIBRA IN THE KITCHEN

Libra is, above all, civilized, sociable, and charming. As a host or hostess, any guest will be welcomed into an environment that is harmonious, pleasant, and balanced. Their symbol is the Scales, so would you expect less? They are master strategists who check every angle to ensure they are on an even keel when the guests arrive.

When Libra sends out an invitation for dinner, be sure to accept right away. It just could be the event of the year, as they are refined, adore beautiful things, and love cultural affairs. Don't be surprised if they have arranged a ballet or operatic performance for your special entertainment during dessert and coffee, or while sipping after-dinner drinks on the veranda.

Should your Libra host or hostess ask what your favorite entrée is, please be specific. If you were to say you love fish, steak, shrimp, and lamb, you may end up with all four. Libras often have a hard time making up their minds, but more than that, they will want you to be happy and will spend hours making all the dishes you love just to see your beaming appreciative smile.

LIBRA GUESTS

When you include Librans on your guest list, expect them to be charming and flit among your other guests, making everyone feel at ease. Nothing will bring a sense of balance to the room like one or two of these gracious creatures. And you, of course, will find them very easy to please—you would never know if they were unhappy anyway!

They will adore a table set with shades of ivory, rose, or pale pink, especially if the fabric has the richness of damask or another elegant linen. Add decorative vases of roses in pink or white both for their beauty and wafting fragrance.

And if you truly want to enchant a Libra, fill little nooks and crannies with delicate violets. A beguiled Libran will certainly provide an enchanted evening for you and your other guests. They haven't earned that reputation of being people pleasers for no reason—they are just born with it!

FEATURED LIBRA WASH-AWAY-THAT-WASTE FOODS

All these foods are great for Libra and the kidneys, but all signs will benefit from the kidney-cleansing properties.

Burrata. High in protein, potassium, magnesium, and phosphorus—known as electrolytes—and vitamins A and C, burrata supports the Libran kidneys. Also low in cholesterol, this variety of mozzarella can be supportive for those with renal issues and others who want or need to avoid cholesterol. Burrata is a nice substitute for other cheeses and one appreciated by Libras who naturally gravitate to the finer things in life. With the goddess Venus as their ruler, what would be more natural?

Cauliflower. These big white heads are very high in vitamins C and K and a good source of the B vitamins, folate, dietary fiber, and potassium. It is beneficial in preventing kidney and bladder cancer. Cauliflower is an excellent food for Libra for keeping the kidneys in tip-top health and fully functioning while they serve it on an elegant platter to please the guest that *loves* cauliflower.

Cherries. Cherries are high in vitamins A and C, both of which are antioxidants and benefit the kidneys. They are also loaded with bioflavonoids that have anti-inflammatory properties. One thing Libras, or any other sign, cannot abide is an inflamed kidney. Even when dried, these dark red beauties are just as interesting and healthy as cranberries for Libra natives, and will be a good substitute in salads, cookies, or as a snack.

Cranberries. Cranberries are very high in vitamin C, and beneficial in preventing urinary tract infections as they make urine more acidic. They contain hippuric acid, antibacterial, and other agents that eliminate *E. coli* bacteria. These red berries prevent kidney and bladder infections, making any Libra's urinary tract happy and well-balanced.

Garlic. Garlic helps fight infections, cancer, and is antibacterial, making it a wonderful addition to dishes for Libras. Faced with their grace and charm, those around Libras won't even notice or mind a bit of "garlic breath." The Libran will smile demurely, pop a stick of gum in his or her mouth, and continue dazzling all the other guests. All other signs should take a hint from Libra and become garlic lovers.

Onions. Onions are antiseptic, antibacterial, and instrumental in squelching *E. coli*. They also prevent urinary tract infections and cystitis. Onions are great all-around for washing away irritants and restoring kidneys and the urinary tract, vital to the health of any Libra, as well as all other signs.

Passion Fruit. These exotic fruits are a good source of vitamins A and C, have trace amounts of vitamin K, and are a natural diuretic that helps wash away toxins that can affect the kidneys. They have properties to cure and prevent urinary tract infections, which affect the kidneys. Plus they are beautiful and sweet, making them desirous to Libras.

Red Bell Peppers. These bright red globes are extremely high in vitamin C and vitamin A. They are exceptionally high in lycopene, actually higher than tomatoes, which helps prevent bladder cancer. Red bell peppers are even better than their green cousins when stuffed, and would make a delicious meal that Libras will gladly prepare for their guests. Any other sign who would like added protection for their kidneys and bladders should ask their Libran friends for that special recipe.

✳

Warm Burrata over Roasted Tomatoes and Basil with Olive Oil and Balsamic Syrup

SERVES 4

This is one of my very favorite recipes! If you haven't tried bur-rata cheese, get to your local Italian grocer as soon as you can, and pick up this piece of heaven.

> 2 pounds plum tomatoes, quartered
>
> ¼ cup olive oil
>
> Kosher salt
>
> 2 tablespoons (¼ stick) unsalted butter, plus 4 tablespoons
> (½ stick), cut in 7 or 8 pieces
>
> 6 garlic cloves, sliced lengthwise
>
> 30 basil leaves, rinsed and dried on paper towels
>
> 1 cup white wine
>
> 4 balls (2.5 ounces) burrata cheese
>
> Extra-virgin olive oil
>
> Fine-quality balsamic syrup (such as Roland brand)

1. Preheat the oven to 400°F.

2. Toss the tomatoes with half of the olive oil and the salt. Place on a rimmed baking sheet and roast for 30 minutes, or until the tomatoes start to blacken around the edges. Remove from the oven and set aside.

3. Place the remaining olive oil and the 2 tablespoons of butter in a heavy-bottomed saucepan over medium-high heat. Add the garlic and sauté until it begins to turn golden, 2 to 3 minutes. Add the roasted tomatoes, basil, and wine and bring to a low boil. Reduce the heat and simmer for 1 hour. Turn off the heat and add the 4 tablespoons of butter pieces, stirring until you reach creamy consistency.

4. Divide the tomatoes evenly among four plates and nest a ball of burrata in the middle of each. Drizzle olive oil and balsamic syrup over the cheese and serve immediately.

Roasted Cauliflower and Maui Onion Gratin with Smoked Gouda

SERVES 12

I have clients who swore they didn't like cauliflower, until they tried this.

2 large heads cauliflower, cut in flowerets

3 large Maui onions, cut in large dice

2 tablespoons olive oil

Kosher salt

4 tablespoons (½ stick) unsalted butter, plus 2 tablespoons
     (¼ stick), melted

4 tablespoons all-purpose flour

3 cups milk

Salt and white pepper

Freshly grated nutmeg

1 cup grated smoked Gouda cheese

1 cup dried bread crumbs

1. Preheat the oven to 400°F.

2. In large bowl, toss together the cauliflower, onion, olive oil, and salt. Transfer to rimmed baking sheets and roast 10 to 15 minutes; do not overcook. Remove from the oven and transfer to a 9 × 13-inch baking dish, sprayed with nonstick cooking spray. Set aside. Reduce the heat to 375°F.

3. In a heavy-bottomed saucepan, combine the butter and flour and cook for 2 to 3 minutes, stirring constantly; do not brown. Slowly add the milk, continuing to stir, until the mixture begins to thicken. Add the salt, pepper, nutmeg, and cheese and stir until the cheese is melted. Pour the sauce over the cauliflower-onion mixture in the baking dish.

4. Add the bread crumbs to the melted butter and mix until crumbly. Sprinkle the topping over the casserole and bake for 10 to 15 minutes until the top is golden brown.

＊

Grilled Cherry and Arugula Salad with Cambozola Cheese
SERVES 4

The sweetness of the cherries with the spiciness of the arugula really make this salad pop!

Vinaigrette
>   2 garlic cloves, peeled and minced
>
>   1 shallot, peeled and minced
>
>   1 teaspoon Dijon mustard
>
>   ½ dried oregano, finely crumbled
>
>   Salt and freshly ground black pepper
>
>   ¼ cup fine-quality balsamic vinegar (such as Villa Manodori)
>
>   ½ cup olive oil

Salad

½ pound dark red cherries, halved and pitted

1 tablespoon olive oil

8 cups arugula

4 ounces Cambozola cheese, crumbled

1. Put the garlic, shallot, mustard, oregano, salt, pepper, and vinegar into the bowl of a food processor and pulse until well blended. With the processor running, gradually add the olive oil in a slow steady stream until the vinaigrette is emulsified. Transfer to a container and refrigerate until ready to use.

2. Preheat a grill to medium heat.

3. Put the arugula in a large salad bowl and set aside.

4. In a medium bowl, toss the cherries with the olive oil. Transfer to a grilling basket and grill for 5 minutes. Add to the arugula and drizzle with the vinaigrette. Toss well.

5. Divide the salad evenly among four salad plates and top with the crumbled cheese. Serve immediately.

Cranberry-Pistachio Scones

MAKES 12 SCONES

These are my grandma Enola's favorites!

2 cups all-purpose flour
1 teaspoon baking soda
¼ cup sugar
½ teaspoon salt
3 tablespoons unsalted butter
1 large egg, beaten
½ cup chopped pistachios
½ cup dried cranberries
1 teaspoon finely grated lemon zest
¾ cup buttermilk

1. Preheat the oven to 400°F.

2. Combine the sifted dry ingredients in a medium bowl. Cut in the butter with a pastry cutter until it resembles small peas.

3. Add the egg, pistachios, cranberries, and lemon zest and mix well. Gradually add the buttermilk to form a thick dough.

4. Turn dough out onto a floured board and knead briefly. Roll out the dough to ¾-inch thickness and using a 2-inch cookie cutter, cut it into 12 rounds. Place the scones on a greased cookie sheet and bake for 15 minutes, or until golden. Serve warm with butter and jam.

✳

Roasted Garlic Mashed Potatoes with Caramelized Onions and Bacon

SERVES 6

Talk about the ultimate comfort food. This is a meal in itself!

> 20 garlic cloves, peeled
>
> Olive oil
>
> Kosher salt
>
> 2½ pounds Yukon gold potatoes, peeled and quartered
>
> 1 tablespoon kosher salt
>
> 4 slices bacon
>
> 1 large Maui onion, peeled and cut into small dice
>
> 4 tablespoons (½ stick) unsalted butter
>
> ¾ cup half-and-half
>
> Salt and freshly ground black pepper

1. Preheat the oven to 350°F.

2. Line a pie plate with aluminum foil and place the garlic in the middle. Drizzle with olive oil and kosher salt. Fold the foil over to form a pouch and seal the top edge. Bake the garlic for 30 minutes. Remove from the oven, cool, and purée immediately.

3. Place the potatoes in a medium pot and cover with cold water. Add the salt and bring to a boil. Reduce the heat and cook until tender.

4. While the potatoes are cooking, fry the bacon in a medium sauté pan until crisp. Transfer the bacon to paper towels to drain and cool. Strain the bacon fat through a fine-mesh strainer into a clean pan. Heat the bacon fat over medium heat. Add the onions to the pan, reduce the heat to low, and cook, stirring every few minutes until the onions are brown and caramelized, about 20 minutes. Crumble the cooled bacon.

5. Add the butter and half-and-half to a small saucepan and place over low heat until the butter is melted. Drain the potatoes and return them to the pot. Using a handheld mixer, begin whipping the potatoes, gradually adding the half-and-half and butter mixture until you reach a creamy consistency. Add the garlic purée and whip to incorporate. Fold in the caramelized onions and the crumbled bacon. Season with salt and pepper to taste.

*

Creamy Five Onion Soup

SERVES 6

I worked in Paris many years ago and I had a French onion soup that I have never forgotten. This is my own version of this classic.

2 tablespoons olive oil

2 tablespoons (¼ stick) unsalted butter

4 Maui onions, cut into medium dice

1 bunch scallions, white part only, sliced

3 shallots, cut into medium dice

3 leeks, white part only, cut in half lengthwise, washed
   thoroughly to remove dirt, sliced in half-rounds

2 tablespoons all-purpose flour

Salt and freshly ground black pepper to taste

½ cup dry sherry

6 cups organic chicken broth

6 fresh thyme sprigs

1 bay leaf

1 cup heavy cream, or more if needed

1 bunch chives, trimmed and cut into chiffonade

6 slices sourdough bread, centers cut into rounds with
   2-inch cookie cutter

6 slices Havarti cheese

1. In a heavy-bottomed pot, heat the olive oil and butter. Add the Maui and scallions, shallots, and leeks and sauté over medium heat until tender. Sprinkle the flour, salt, and pepper over the onions and stir. Deglaze the pan with the sherry and add the chicken broth, thyme sprigs, and bay leaf. Simmer for 30 minutes.

2. Remove and discard the thyme sprigs and bay leaf. Add the cream and simmer. Stir in the chives.

3. Preheat the oven to broil. Ladle the soup into six 10-ounce ramekins or individual soup tureens. Place a bread round in each and top with a cheese slice. Place the ramekins under the broiler until the cheese is melted and browned. Serve immediately.

Creamy Roasted Red Pepper Sauce with Italian Sausage over Fusilli

SERVES 8

This is great on those nights when you just want to throw something together and relax with a glass of red wine.

> 2 roasted red bell peppers, skinned, seeded, and cut into
>   large dice
> 1 large onion, chopped
> 3 garlic cloves, chopped
> 2 tablespoons (¼ stick) unsalted butter
> 2 tablespoons olive oil
> Leaves from ½ bunch basil
> Juice of ½ lemon
> 1 pound Italian sausage, removed from casing
> Hot red pepper flakes
> 1 cup heavy cream
> 1 pound fusilli pasta
> 1 cup grated Parmigiano-Reggiano cheese

1. Wash two red bell peppers and char skins on a grill at medium-high heat. Turn peppers a few times to ensure all sides are charred. Place the peppers in a ziplock bag and allow them to cool. When they are cool enough to touch, slip off the charred skin, remove the membranes and seeds, and chop into a large dice.

2. In a heavy-bottomed pot, heat the butter and olive oil. Add the onion and garlic and sauté until translucent and tender. Add the basil and roasted bell peppers and simmer until the basil is wilted. Transfer the mixture to a food processor, add the lemon juice, and purée.

3. In a sauté pan, break up the sausage meat, season with red pepper flakes, and brown. Drain the excess fat. Stir in the purée. Slowly whisk in the cream until you reach the desired consistency.

4. To a large pot of rapidly boiling salted water, add the fusilli and cook for 8 minutes, or until al dente. Drain and place in a large serving bowl and toss with the sauce. Garnish with cheese, and serve.

Coconut- and Macadamia Nut–Crusted Shrimp with Lilikoi Cocktail Sauce

SERVES 4

This is a big-time crowd-pleaser! Men, women, children! They can't get enough!

> 12 extra-large U-8 shrimp
> 1 cup all-purpose flour
> Sea salt
> 1 cup panko bread crumbs
> ½ cup sweetened, shredded coconut
> ½ cup finely chopped macadamia nuts
> 4 large eggs
> 1 cup favorite cocktail sauce
> 1 tablespoon lilikoi (passion fruit) purée
> 2 cups peanut oil

1. In a bowl, mix together the flour and salt. In a separate bowl combine the panko, coconut, and macadamia nuts. Beat the eggs in another bowl. Dredge the shrimp in the flour, dip into the egg, and coat with the panko mix so the shrimp are completely coated. Line the shrimp up on a baking sheet and place in the freezer for 30 minutes.

2. In a small bowl, mix together the cocktail sauce and lilikoi purée. Cover and refrigerate.

3. Heat the oil to 375°F. Line a baking sheet with paper towels. Deep-fry the shrimp, in batches, until golden brown. Remove from the oil with a stainless steel skimmer and transfer to the lined baking sheet. Serve the shrimp warm with the cocktail sauce.

8
Scorpio

October 23–November 21

GET-YOU-IN-THE-MOOD FOODS

All these foods have been carefully selected for Scorpio, as this sign rules the reproductive organs. These foods are all aphrodisiacs, God's perfect foods for the most sensuous, sultry, and expressive of all signs. Scorpio must feel passionate about all their undertakings or their interest wanes. These foods will fill the need on all levels. All other signs that are feeling less than frisky, or need help in that department, can benefit from these foods.

Symbol: Scorpion, eagle, snake, and the mythical phoenix
Ruling Planet: Pluto
Body Part Ruled: Reproductive organs
House Ruled: Eighth, the house of birth, death, regeneration, and sex

Element: Water
Color: Scarlet
Stone: Topaz
Key Phrase: I desire
Trait: Idealism
Quality: Fixed

Scorpio is ruled by the mysterious planet Pluto and rules the eighth house, the house of birth, death, regeneration, and transformation. The eighth house also rules sex and Scorpio is certainly the sexiest sign of the zodiac and one of the most passionate. The Scorpio sign rules the reproductive organs, which may explain the sexy reputation. It should come as no surprise that many of the foods found in this chapter are natural aphrodisiacs!

The scorpion is the traditional symbol of the sign, along with the eagle and the snake. But the less recognized symbol is the phoenix, the mythical bird said to burst into flames at death and be reborn out of the ashes to rise again in splendor. Scorpios have this same unique ability, more so than any other sign. When they crash and burn, they are able to regenerate and arise, renewed, from the ashes of their failures or defeats, to soar again. They can quite literally reinvent themselves over and over again throughout their lives.

SCORPIO IN THE KITCHEN

Scorpios rarely let anyone see too deeply into their psyche, preferring to keep their innermost self a secret. Though you may feel that you never quite get to know the "real" person, don't expect to remain incognito yourself. A Scorpio's intense investigative and scrutinizing abilities can make the most secretive person reveal the skeletons in their closet, so you may as well 'fess up about your vices, be they dark chocolates, champagne, foie gras, or after-dinner cigars. Scorpio *will* find out!

They are intrigued by mystery and the mystical, so when you accept a dinner invitation from your Scorpio friend expect the meal to be an almost spiritual event. Scorpios don't like surprises themselves, but delight in surprising you, so even though they have gotten you to spill the beans and you may think you know exactly what is coming, be prepared! Your special treat will be served with such mystique and finesse that you will be completely blindsided and blown away. It will be an evening to remember as you succumb to your passionate side!

SCORPIO GUESTS

There's no better friend to have than a Scorpio. Loyal to a fault, they never forget a kindness and will reciprocate at a moment's notice. Though known for their serious, intense side, Scorpios also have a great sense of humor and can be the life of the party. You will know your Scorpio guest has arrived even before you see him or her—that trademark laugh is recognizable anywhere. And when they're "on," you'll find them surrounded by adoring admirers captivated by those sensuous eyes and that mysterious smile. They will keep your other guests occupied while you put the finishing touches on dinner!

When planning your menu, be warned: don't prepare only aphrodisiacs as that could be dangerous! One nice aphrodisiac entrée will suffice unless this is an intimate dinner for you and your Scorpio invitee, but more on that later. Accompany the meal with a goblet of red wine, which is one of Scorpio's favorites. Serve dinner in an exquisite, romantic setting—white linen tablecloth, scarlet napkins (Scorpio's color), and an assortment of candles in different sizes and in hues of gold, crimson, and cream.

Add a centerpiece of gardenias—one of Scorpio's flowers—floating in a crystal bowl and you will have a most delighted Scorpio on your hands. Since they play everything close to the vest, you may not realize just how thrilled they are, but trust me, they will be!

As the host or hostess for a Scorpio friend, you have just learned how to properly entertain one of these sexy creatures, but what about entertaining that special someone in your life? Tune in to your inner Scorpio by exploring your more sensual self with a host of aphrodisiac foods and ingredients—and prepare a romantic meal you'll never forget!

Or better yet, create an ambiance in front of the fire on a plush rug, sprinkle rose petals from the front door to the fire, and feed each other, using only your own hands to deliver each bite to your lover's lips. Scorpio loves the mysterious, so you might use a blindfold to add to his or her pleasure, which also makes this tasty experience that much more potent. Turn the stereo to Ravel's "Bolero" and let the evening begin!

FEATURED SCORPIO GET-YOU-IN-THE-MOOD FOODS

All these foods are great for Scorpio and the libido, but all signs will benefit from the aphrodisiac, mood-enhancing properties.

Asparagus. Asparagus provides vitamin E, calcium, potassium, and phosphorus to the improved creation of hormones and a healthy urinary tract. The Doctrine of Signatures, an early medical concept, says that if one thing bears a resemblance to another, it is said to benefit that which it resembles. So it is only natural that the phallic silhouette of asparagus should benefit the prowess of Scorpio or other signs that are in the mood.

Caviar. Caviar is very high in zinc, which enhances the prowess of males. It aids the production of testosterone, keeping levels ready for romance. This may well be the perfect appetizer to serve to your Scorpio lover to get him in the mood, or for any other sign that needs a little prodding.

Chocolate. Dating back to the Aztecs, chocolate has been purported to be an aphrodisiac. There is a scientific explanation for this, having to do with tryptophan, serotonin, falling in love, and the brain, but it is clinical and far less romantic than the actual experience. When it comes to chocolate, any decisions need to be made experientially. There is nothing like that first bite of decadent, sensuous creaminess as it bursts on your tongue! Except sharing it with your lover! And the best news is that dark chocolate is good for you with its antioxidant properties. So go ahead, you've been given permission to indulge!

Figs. In ancient times, an open fig was thought to resemble female sexual organs, which was visually stimulating. Eating a ripe fig with your hands or, even better, feeding one to your mate is a sensual act. Ancient Romans thought they were a gift from Bacchus, the god of fertility.

Ginger. In the *Kama Sutra,* ginger has actually been documented to be an aphrodisiac in the section on rituals. This may be why Madame Bovary used it as a concoction for all her lovers. Even today, listed under health benefits, one can find that ginger may be better for men than Viagra. Ginger can also generate a feeling of happiness and euphoria. Maybe Scorpios and all signs should keep a big knob of ginger in their kitchens for regular addition to their favorite recipes.

Honey. Honey was the source of many remedies to cure impotence and enhance virility in ancient Egypt. In medieval times, mead, which was made from honey, was considered a seductive drink for newly married couples that would entice them into the marriage bed.

Oysters. These mollusks date to ancient Roman times as an aphrodisiac, when oysters were considered to be the perfect food to ply women with to increase their libidos. They were also thought to resemble female sex organs, which would arouse males as they fed tender bites to their lovers. Any sign wishing for a night filled with romance should head to the local fishmonger.

Strawberries. What could be a more perfect food for love than this token of Venus? Legend has it that Venus wept so much at the death of Adonis that her tears turned into the heart-shaped strawberry to immortalize their love. Strawberries are high in vitamin C and are delectable dipped in whipped cream, chocolate, or brown sugar–flavored sour cream and shared with your lover. Another reported version is to serve white port with wild strawberries, which will provide very powerful results for Scorpio.

✳

Grilled Asparagus with Black Truffle Oil

SERVES 4

Growing up in the Sacramento Valley, asparagus was abundant and one of my favorites. This is a preparation that has become a family favorite and is always a big hit, as I hope it will be when you serve it to your family and friends.

> 1 pound asparagus
> 1 tablespoon olive oil
> Kosher salt
> 2 tablespoons black truffle oil
> ½ teaspoon finely grated lemon zest
> Juice of ½ lemon

1. Wash and trim the asparagus. Toss with olive oil and salt.
2. Preheat a grill to medium-high heat. Place the asparagus in a grill basket or a fish rack. Cook for a few minutes on each side until the asparagus is marked and tender. Remove from the grill and place in a baking dish. Drizzle with truffle

oil and lemon juice. Place on a serving platter and garnish
with the lemon zest.

*

Caviar Party for Two

*There is nothing like a private caviar party with a cold bottle of
Champagne! I did a classic caviar setup for my daughter and a
couple of friends the night before she left for college. It was the
first time she had ever experienced caviar, and boy, have I created a monster!*

Crème Fraîche

> ½ cup heavy cream
> ½ cup sour cream

Blinis

> ¼ cup buckwheat flour
> ¾ cup all-purpose flour
> ½ teaspoon baking powder
> ½ teaspoon salt
> 1 teaspoon sugar
> ¾ cup buttermilk
> 2 large eggs
> 8 tablespoons (1 stick) unsalted butter, melted, separated
> > into 2 tablespoons and remaining amount

Condiments

> 4 shallots, finely minced
>
> 4 hard-boiled egg yolks, minced
>
> 4 hard-boiled egg whites, minced
>
> 2 ounces capers
>
> 1 cup crème fraîche
>
> 2 ounces Osetra caviar

1. To make the crème fraîche, whisk the heavy cream and sour cream together in a small bowl, cover, and refrigerate for at least 2 hours.

2. Sift together the flours, baking powder, salt, and sugar into a bowl. Set aside.

3. Whisk together the buttermilk, eggs, and 2 tablespoons of the butter. Add the flour mixture a quarter at a time and beat well.

4. Heat a griddle and spray with nonstick spray. Drop batter onto the griddle in one-tablespoon increments. Cook the blini on each side until golden. Transfer to a plate and cool. Continue making blinis until all the batter is used. The blinis can be made a day or two ahead of time and stored in an airtight container, but are always best fresh off the griddle.

5. Transfer the condiments to individual small bowls. Open the caviar, leaving it in its original container, and serve on a platter of ice with a small mother-of-pearl spoon. Silver or silverplate spoons will oxidize and impart a metallic flavor to the caviar.

6. Serve the blinis warm in a basket wrapped in a napkin. Serve with condiments and caviar, building your own combination of flavors.

*

Chocolate-Rum Pot de Crème

SERVES 8

Living in the Tropics for almost twenty years, I have become a big fan of dark rum. This is a combination of two of my favorites.

    4 ounces bittersweet chocolate, chopped

    3 cups heavy cream

    ¼ cup dark rum

    6 large egg yolks

    ¾ cups granulated sugar

    1 vanilla bean, split lengthwise, seeds scraped

    1 cup heavy cream

    ¼ cup brown sugar

    ½ teaspoon pure vanilla extract

    2 ounces shaved chocolate

1. Preheat the oven to 300°F.

2. Put the chopped chocolate in a bowl. Mix the cream,

rum, vanilla seeds, and the vanilla pod in a medium heavy-bottomed saucepan and place over medium heat until scalding. Pour the mixture over the chocolate in the bowl, remove the vanilla pod, and whisk the mixture until smooth.

3. In a separate bowl, whisk together the yolks and granulated sugar. Temper the egg mixture with the warm chocolate mixture. Then return to the stovetop over medium heat to thicken slightly and until it coats the back of a wooden spoon.

4. Divide the custard equally among eight 4-ounce ramekins. Place the ramekins in a roasting pan and pour in water to come halfway up the sides of the ramekins. Bake for 40 to 45 minutes until the custards are almost set but still a bit jiggly in the center. Remove from the water bath and let cool for 30 minutes, then put in the refrigerator and chill for at least 4 hours.

5. Just before serving, whip the cream, brown sugar, and vanilla extract until stiff peaks form. Serve the pots de crème with a dollop of whipped cream and garnish with the shaved chocolate.

Pancetta-Wrapped Figs with Gorgonzola

SERVES 6

When I was growing up we had a fig tree in our backyard and when it was in season, we had an abundance of this beautiful fruit. Mom would make jam and breads. This is another wonderful way to enjoy these gems!

12 large fresh black mission figs, trimmed and halved
     lengthwise
12 slices pancetta
2 ounces Gorgonzola cheese, cut into 12 pieces
Honey

1. Preheat the oven to broil.

2. Wrap each fig half with pancetta and secure with a toothpick. Spray a baking sheet with nonstick cooking spray and arrange the figs on the pan. Broil on both sides until the pancetta is browned.

3. Top each fig with a piece of cheese and drizzle with a couple drops of honey. Return the pan to the oven and broil just long enough to soften the cheese. Serve immediately.

✳

Triple Ginger Chocolate Shortbread Cookies

MAKES 3 DOZEN COOKIES

Love, love, love! What more can I say? These are perfect for feeding to that special someone!

3 cups all-purpose flour

1 teaspoon ground ginger

16 tablespoons (2 sticks) unsalted butter

¾ cup confectioners' sugar

1 tablespoon peeled and finely minced fresh ginger

1 cup minced chocolate-covered crystallized ginger

1. In a bowl, mix together the flour and ground ginger. Set aside.

2. In the bowl of an electric mixer, cream together the butter, sugar, and fresh and crystallized gingers at medium speed. Add the flour a little at a time, and mix until fully incorporated.

3. Shape the dough into a log and wrap it in plastic wrap. Continue shaping the log into a long rectangle with even sides. Chill the log in the freezer for 2 hours.

4. Preheat the oven to 300°F.

5. Slice the chilled log into ½-inch-thick cookies. Place on greased cookie sheets 2 inches apart and bake for 20 to 25 minutes or until lightly golden. Let cool for 5 minutes on the baking sheet, then transfer to a wire rack to cool completely.

*

Asian Honey Chicken Kabobs

SERVES 4

These are a perfect finger food to hand-feed your loved one, one bite at a time! In a less intimate surrounding, they make a great appetizer. Or accompany with a nice veggie stir-fry and rice for a complete dinner.

Kabobs

>   1 pound boneless, skinless chicken thighs, cut in 1-inch
>   cubes

Marinade

>   ¼ cup low-sodium soy sauce
>   ¼ cup honey
>   ¼ cup freshly squeezed orange juice
>   1 teaspoon sesame oil
>   2 tablespoons dry sherry
>   3 garlic cloves, finely minced
>   1 teaspoon peeled and finely minced fresh ginger
>   ¼ teaspoon hot red pepper flakes
>   2 scallions, chopped

½ fresh pineapple, peeled and cut into 1-inch cubes

Twelve 6- to 8-inch bamboo skewers

1. Place the cubed chicken in a glass baking dish.

2. Combine all the ingredients for the marinade in a bowl and mix well. Pour the marinade over the chicken, cover with plastic wrap, and refrigerate for at least 2 hours or overnight.

3. Soak the bamboo skewers in water for 30 minutes before grilling. Remove the chicken from the refrigerator and skewer the chicken cubes, alternating them with the pineapple chunks to make the kabobs.

4. Preheat a grill to 400°F. Grill the chicken kabobs for 5 minutes on each side, or until the chicken is cooked through. Transfer to a serving platter and serve immediately.

✳

Malpeque Oysters on the Half Shell with Ginger Mignonette Sauce

SERVES 2

If you have never eaten oysters on the half shell, this is a great way to start. They are light bodied, with a clean and sweet finish. My daughter and I can eat several dozen of these with no problem.

Mignonette Sauce

>   2 tablespoons finely minced shallot
>
>   ½ teaspoon mixed red and white peppercorns, coarsely
>   ground
>
>   ½ cup seasoned rice wine vinegar
>
>   Juice of ½ lemon

Oysters

>   Small bag crushed ice
>
>   1 lemon, ends trimmed, cut into 8 lengthwise slices
>
>   1 dozen fresh Malpeque oysters

1. One to two days before serving the oysters, whisk all the mignonette ingredients together in a bowl and store in the refrigerator to allow the blending of flavors.

2. On the day of serving, prepare a serving platter with crushed ice and store it in the freezer so it will be ready upon cleaning and shucking oysters.

3. Check the oysters to make sure they are tightly closed and alive. If any oyster opens on its own, it is dead, and must be discarded. Under cold running water, scrub each oyster thoroughly with a brush to remove any dirt or grit.

4. Be sure to have the proper equipment—an oyster knife— before beginning to shuck oysters. (These can be purchased at any culinary store and most fish markets.) Hold an oyster in your hand cupped side down in a towel to avoid cutting yourself on the sharp shell. Working over a bowl to catch any juices, slip the point of the knife between the shells close to the hinge. Twist the knife like turning a doorknob to release the muscle.

5. Scrape the flesh in the top shell into the bottom shell and discard the top shell. Use the knife to release the oyster. Check to see if there is any grit under the oyster, and if so remove it.

6. Pour the mignonette sauce into a small bowl or ramekin. Remove the platter of ice from the freezer, place the bowl of sauce in the center, and place a small spoon in the bowl. Nestle the oysters in the ice and garnish the platter with lemon slices. Serve immediately.

✳

Strawberry Rose Petal Cupcakes with Rose Butter Cream Frosting

MAKES 12 CUPCAKES

This is one sure way to serve aphrodisiac strawberries that will grab the attention of that special someone. What great fun it will be to feed each other these sumptuous treats right out of your hand!

Candied Rose Petals

    24 unsprayed rose petals

    Organic pasteurized egg whites

    1/3 cup superfine sugar

Cupcakes

    1 1/4 cups all-purpose flour

    1/2 teaspoon baking powder

    1/4 teaspoon baking soda

    1/4 teaspoon salt

    1/4 cup canola oil

    1 cup granulated sugar

    3 large egg whites, slightly beaten

    1/4 teaspoon pure vanilla extract

    1 teaspoon rose water

    1/2 cup sour cream

    1/2 cup crushed strawberries

Butter Cream Frosting

    8 tablespoons (1 stick) unsalted butter

    3 to 4 cups confectioners' sugar

    1/4 cup whole milk

    1 teaspoon pure vanilla extract

    1 teaspoon rose water

1. To make the candied rose petals, wash 24 unsprayed, deep red rose petals and set aside on paper towels to dry.

2. When dry, transfer to a baking sheet lined with parchment paper. Brush the petals with organic pasteurized egg whites on both sides. Sprinkle with superfine sugar until well coated. Allow to dry thoroughly. Set aside.

3. Preheat the oven to 350°F.

4. Sift all the dry ingredients into a small bowl and set aside.

5. Cream the oil and sugar in a mixing bowl with a handheld mixer. Add the egg whites and beat lightly. Add vanilla, rose water, and sour cream and beat lightly. Add the crushed strawberries and mix lightly until incorporated.

6. Add the dry ingredients to the wet ingredients and mix thoroughly. Divide the batter equally among 12 wells of a cupcake pan and bake for 15 to 20 minutes until a toothpick inserted in the center comes out clean. Transfer to a wire rack to cool completely.

7. While the cupcakes cool, make the frosting. In the bowl of an electric mixer, beat the butter until fluffy. Add the sugar and cream together. Add the milk, vanilla, and rose water and beat until smooth. When the cupcakes are cool, frost and top each with two candied rose petals.

Sagittarius

November 22–December 21

BREAK-DOWN-THAT-FAT FOODS

These foods were selected for Sagittarius as this sign rules the liver. They are all liver cleansing and detoxifying to keep the Sagittarian liver functioning at the maximum so he or she can be off on the latest adventure. And if they aren't travelling, they will most likely be entertaining their friends and families with the newest joke and their famous sense of humor.

Symbol: The Archer
Ruling Planet: Jupiter
Body Part Ruled: Liver
House Ruled: Ninth, the house of religion, knowledge, higher education, and travel

Element: Fire
Color: Purple
Stone: Turquoise
Key Phrase: I see
Trait: Optimism
Quality: Mutable

Sagittarius and its ruler, Jupiter, rule the ninth house of higher education, travel, religion, and knowledge. Sagittarians tend to be philosophical, intelligent, idealistic, and enthusiastic. Everything they do is on a grand scale in their search to gain knowledge, explore the world, or excel at their chosen sport. They have such great drive for adventure and extraordinary quest, making them the ultimate travelers of the zodiac.

Highly ambitious and focused, with an ability to assimilate large amounts of information quickly, they have great vision and usually succeed in their endeavors. They dislike any kind of confinement or rigidity, preferring a freer environment in which to bring their ideas to fruition. With Jupiter as the ruling planet, they are naturally lucky; this may explain why money is not the primary goal in any undertaking, but a resource that seems to be there when they need it.

SAGITTARIUS IN THE KITCHEN

When you accept an invitation for dinner at your Sagittarius friend's home, expect a divine meal from exotic ports of call they have visited on their sojourns as the zodiac's greatest travelers. They have been to more places on the planet than any other sign. Like their Archer symbol, also known as the centaur—half human and half horse—they love the outdoors and the freedom it offers, and Sagittarians love their freedom. Sags are restless for that next adventure waiting around the corner, but given the freedom to climb the most dangerous mountain, test drive the next supercar, or travel to their most beloved spot on the globe, they will always come running home when the mission is complete.

Above all, the Sagittarian finds the journey most intriguing. The absolute most intriguing Archer's trek is anywhere they get a rush, be it climbing Mount Kilimanjaro, rafting the Amazon, or diving the Great Barrier Reef. Part of the adventure is indulging in all the unusual foods from each place, adding it to their cuisine repertoire to prepare for family and friends as soon as they return home.

Sags will want the evening to begin in the kitchen where they can amuse their guests with tall tales as they toss in a pinch of this and that to the large pot simmering away on the stove. You will soon think your friend has lost track of the recipe, but not to worry, he doesn't use one, but cooks from a place of intuition. All those spices and other ingredients will come together and you will be feasting on such delicious fare you will feel transported to faraway places!

SAGITTARIUS GUESTS

Archers are the heart and soul of a dinner party as they long for all things social. Not only that, they make lively company and will keep all your other guests entertained with wild stories of their latest hair-raising trip, be it climbing one of the most dangerous peaks in the Himalayas or trekking across the Sahara. When they run out of stories, if that is possible, they will engage their highly developed sense of humor and keep your guests laughing until dinner is served.

Sags are also known to eat anything unusual that other signs are afraid to try, so when planning your menu for any Sagittarians, all options are open. Play Sag for an evening and try something new that you've not prepared before. Don't worry that your other guests won't like it. Your appreciative Sagittarius guest will most certainly cajole everyone else into trying it and, most important, loving it. These creatures are the ones that can sell ice to Eskimos!

Depending on the season, you can select the perfect place to serve your feast. On a perfectly beautiful day, gather the food, utensils, and appetite and head outdoors. There's nothing a Sagittarian loves more than a picnic, except maybe an old-fashioned barbecue, where you will soon find him or her offering to help with grilling the entrée as they love to be interactive.

If the weather doesn't cooperate, don't stress; move the picnic to your family room. Throw large cushions in shades of purple or turquoise in front of the fireplace for everyone to sit on. Put the tablecloth on the floor and serve your delighted Sag friend right there. Finish by toasting marshmallows over the roaring fire and make s'mores for dessert. Any Sagittarian will *love* this adventure!

FEATURED SAGITTARIUS
BREAK-DOWN-THAT-FAT FOODS

All these foods are great for Sagittarius and the liver, but all signs will benefit from the liver-cleansing properties.

Apples. Apples improve elimination of toxicants and facilitate digestion. The peels of Braeburns are said to have concentrations of UVB protection, which will defend Sagittarian adventurers and other outdoor types from harsh sun rays. Antioxidants, enzymes, and fiber are also present to keep the liver well tuned.

Avocado. Avocados contain glutathione, which reacts as an antioxidant and can rev up a sluggish liver. The monounsaturated and polyunsaturated fats in avocados are healthy fats that do not damage the liver. There is some evidence

that symptoms of alcoholic liver disease will respond to avocado consumption. So Sagittarians can certainly benefit
from a scoop or two of guacamole or slices of avocado on
their sandwiches.

Beets. Beets with their excellent blood-cleansing characteristics aid the functioning of the liver, which is ruled by
Sagittarius. The high-iron, potassium, calcium, and mineral
content facilitates the building of liver cells. Anyone with
that sluggish feeling in need of cleansing can turn to beets
to perk up the liver. Beets are naturally sweet and can appease the sweet tooth of Sagittarians and other signs.

Cinnamon. Not only has cinnamon been used as a spice for
centuries, but it is also medicinal with anti-inflammatory,
antibacterial, and antimicrobial properties. Research shows
that cinnamon is beneficial for Type II diabetes as it aids in
lowering blood sugar. The addition of this spice on a regular
basis may ensure better liver health no matter which sign
one is.

Coconut. Coconut has anti-inflammatory properties that
are beneficial for the liver and pancreas, and work in conjunction for regulating blood sugar. Coconut is also an antioxidant and aids in detoxification, making it perfect for the
Sagittarius native and all other signs. It also has antiaging

properties, so Sags, and all other signs who wish to stay forever young, need to indulge.

Halibut. Selenium content is a necessary part of glutathione peroxidase, the critical antioxidant for liver detoxification and cleansing. Eating halibut at least once a week will promote a healthy liver for all signs, but especially for Sags.

Meyer Lemons. Meyer lemon juice is especially good for liver flushing and proper functioning. It is recommended to drink freshly squeezed lemon juice in hot water every day as a liver tonic to help produce bile for processing ingested foods. This might be better for Sagittarians than lemonade, but any way Meyer lemons are prepared will be beneficial. So lemon bars, lemonade, lemon water, bring them on!

Rocket. These bitter greens, originally thought to be a pesky weed, are packed with vitamins A and K, potassium, and calcium, all of which promote liver detoxification and the treatment of jaundice, making them an excellent choice for Sagittarians and all other signs needing a liver flush. Forget the health roundup; use the tender leaves in your next salad!

✳

Apple Crisp à la Mode

SERVES 12

This is my grandma's recipe. Love you, Gram!

Apples

> 8 Granny Smith apples, peeled, cored, and sliced
>
> 1 teaspoon ground cinnamon
>
> ½ teaspoon freshly grated nutmeg
>
> Pinch of ground cloves
>
> ½ cup all-purpose flour
>
> 1 ⅓ cups granulated sugar
>
> ¼ cup apple brandy
>
> 4 tablespoons (½ stick) unsalted butter, cut in small pieces

Crisp

> ½ cup firmly packed light brown sugar
>
> ½ cup sugar
>
> 1 cup all-purpose flour
>
> 1 cup rolled oats
>
> ½ cup pecans, chopped to a mealy consistency
>
> 1 tablespoon baking powder plus 1 teaspoon
>
> 6 tablespoons (¾ stick) unsalted butter
>
> 1 large egg, beaten

1. Preheat the oven to 350°F.

2. In a large bowl, combine all the ingredients for the apples except the butter. Mix thoroughly and transfer to a 13×9-inch baking dish, sprayed with nonstick cooking spray. Dot with the butter pieces and set aside.

3. In another large bowl, mix all the ingredients for the crumble except the butter and egg. Add the butter and mix with your hands or a pastry cutter until the butter is the size of small peas. Add the egg and mix; the mixture should still be crumbly and slightly wet. Crumble over the apple mixture.

4. Bake for 45 minutes, or until golden and crisp. Serve with vanilla ice cream and *Cinnamon Sauce*.

Lobster Guacamole

SERVES 8

Two of my favorite foods ever, combined into one! To die for!

  4 avocados, peeled, pitted

  ½ cup finely minced red onion

  1 jalapeño, seeds and membrane removed, finely minced

  3 garlic cloves, finely minced

  ½ cup minced, fresh cilantro plus sprigs for garnish

  ¼ cup mayonnaise

Juice of 1 lime
Garlic salt
Salt and freshly ground black pepper
½ pound cooked lobster meat, chopped
1 lime, cut into wedges for garnish

1. Mash the avocado with a masher in a medium bowl just until chunky. Add all the remaining ingredients except for the lobster, cilantro sprigs, and lime wedges, and mix well. Fold in the lobster meat.

2. Transfer the guacamole to a serving bowl and garnish with the lime wedges and cilantro sprigs. Chill for 1 hour before serving.

Warm Baby Beet Salad over Grilled Portobellos with Brie

SERVES 4

Such a great warm winter salad!

> Salt
> 1 bunch of baby beets (4 to 5), cleaned and trimmed
> 3 tablespoons olive oil
> 2 red onions, thinly sliced into rounds
> 2 tablespoons fine balsamic vinegar
> ½ teaspoon Dijon mustard
> 4 medium portobello mushrooms, stems trimmed
> 4 ounces Brie cheese

1. Place the beets in a pot, cover with cold salted water, and boil until tender. Drain and slip off the skins as soon as the beets are cool enough to handle, and cut into a medium dice. Set aside.

2. In a heavy-bottomed pot or large sauté pan, heat 2 tablespoons of the olive oil over medium-high heat. Add the onions, reduce the heat, and sauté, stirring every few minutes until the onions are caramelized. Add the beets and reheat. Deglaze the pan with the balsamic vinegar. Add the Dijon and mix well.

3. Preheat a grill to medium high. Brush each portobello mushroom with the remaining 1 tablespoon of olive oil and grill over indirect heat until tender, about 10 minutes. Remove from the grill and place gill side up on a baking sheet. Evenly distribute the beet and onion mixture among the mushrooms. Top each with 1 ounce Brie, and place under a broiler until the Brie is melted and bubbly. Serve immediately.

✳

Cinnamon Sauce

YIELDS 3 CUPS

This will bring apple pie to an all new high!

> 2 cups firmly packed light brown sugar
>
> 2 tablespoons all-purpose flour
>
> 1 ½ cups water
>
> ½ cup apple juice or cider
>
> 1 vanilla bean, split lengthwise, seeds scraped
>
> 1 ½ teaspoons ground cinnamon
>
> 4 tablespoons (½ stick) unsalted butter

1. Mix together the sugar and flour in a saucepan. Slowly stir in the water and apple juice or cider, until the sugar and flour are dissolved. Add the vanilla pod, scraped seeds, and the cinnamon and simmer gently until slightly thickened, stirring continually.

2. Add butter and cook for 6 to 8 minutes more. Remove from the heat and discard the vanilla pod. Scoop over *Apple Crisp à la Mode* or French toast.

✳

Chocolate-Dipped Coconut Biscotti

MAKES 45 BISCOTTI

Great with your morning joe or your afternoon tea!

> 2 cups all-purpose flour
>
> 1 ½ teaspoons baking powder
>
> ½ teaspoon salt
>
> 1 cup sugar
>
> 8 tablespoons (1 stick) unsalted butter, softened
>
> 1 teaspoon almond extract
>
> 2 large eggs
>
> 2 cups sweetened flaked coconut
>
> ½ cup chopped, blanched, slivered almonds
>
> 2 cups semisweet chocolate chunks

1. Preheat the oven to 350°F.

2. In a medium bowl, mix together the sifted flour, baking powder, and salt and set aside.

3. Cream the sugar and butter together in the bowl of an electric mixer on medium speed. Add the almond extract and eggs and beat well. Reduce the speed to low, add the coconut, and mix in.

4. Gradually add the flour mixture and mix well. Add the nuts and mix in. Divide the dough into 3 equal pieces. If sticky, dust with a bit of flour. Form the dough into 12-inch loaves and place on cookie sheets lined with parchment paper. Bake for 20 to 25 minutes.

5. Remove from the oven and transfer the loaves to a wire cooling rack. When cool, transfer to a cutting board and slice each loaf, on the diagonal, into ½-inch-wide slices.

6. Place the sliced cookies on the cookie sheets and bake 12 to 15 minutes to toast. Transfer to a wire rack.

7. Melt the chocolate in a small saucepan over low heat. When the biscotti are cool, dip half of each piece into the melted chocolate and place on parchment paper to allow the chocolate to cool.

Pesto-Crusted Halibut with Tomato, Olive, and Caper Relish

SERVES 4

This is one of my favorite ways to serve fish. It easily adapts to salmon, snapper, sea bass, or whatever is your favorite fish.

Relish

　　4 plum tomatoes, seeded and diced

　　1 cup pitted Kalamata olives, chopped

　　¼ cup capers

　　1 garlic clove, finely minced

　　1 tablespoon olive oil

　　Juice of 1 Meyer lemon

　　Salt and freshly ground black pepper

Halibut

　　2 tablespoons olive oil

　　Four 6-ounce halibut fillets

　　¾ cup favorite pesto

　　2 Meyer lemons, cut in wedges for garnish

1. Preheat the oven to 300°F. In a large mixing bowl, combine the ingredients for the relish. Mix well and set aside.

2. Coat one side of each halibut fillet with pesto. Heat 1 tablespoon of olive oil in a heavy-bottomed sauté pan. Add the halibut, pesto side down, and sear until a crust forms and is crisp. Coat the top side of the fish with pesto and, using tongs, carefully squeeze the sides of the fillets to pick them up and turn them over, not disturbing the crust. Sear on the second side using the remaining tablespoon of olive oil, if necessary. Transfer the fish from the pan to a baking dish and finish in the oven for 15 minutes.

3. Transfer the fillets to four individual plates. Serve with the relish and garnish with Meyer lemon wedges. *Meyer Lemon Orzo Risotto* (recipe follows) is a perfect accompaniment.

Meyer Lemon Orzo Risotto

SERVES 8

Delicious with the halibut!

> 2 tablespoons (¼ stick) unsalted butter
>
> 2 tablespoons olive oil
>
> ½ cup minced shallots
>
> 1 pound orzo pasta
>
> ¼ cup Madeira wine
>
> 5 cups chicken broth
>
> 1 cup Parmigiano-Reggiano cheese
>
> 8 ounces mascarpone cheese
>
> 1 tablespoon finely grated Meyer lemon zest
>
> 2 tablespoons freshly squeezed Meyer lemon juice
>
> ½ cup finely chopped parsley
>
> ½ cup feta cheese

1. In a saucepan, bring the chicken broth to a boil. Remove from the heat and cover. In a heavy-bottomed pot, melt the butter with the olive oil over medium heat. Add shallots and sauté until tender. Add the orzo and stir constantly until the orzo is golden brown, about 5 minutes. Deglaze the pan with the Madeira and continue stirring.

2. Begin adding the hot chicken broth, one ladleful at a time, stirring continuously. Add each additional ladleful just before the broth from the previous ladleful is completely absorbed. Continue in this manner until the orzo is tender and creamy. **3.** Add the Parmesan and mascarpone cheeses, lemon zest, lemon juice, and chopped parsley, and stir until the cheeses are melted and well blended. Sprinkle a little feta on top of each serving when plating. Serve with *Pesto-Crusted Halibut with Tomato, Olive, and Caper Relish*.

Pasta Arrabbiata with Shrimp, Arugula, and Grana Padano

SERVES 8

This dish is so easy to make, but will have your guests thinking you slaved in the kitchen for hours.

> Salt
>
> 1 pound penne pasta

Sauce

> 2 pounds plum tomatoes, cored
>
> 2 tablespoons olive oil
>
> 2 tablespoons (¼ stick) unsalted butter
>
> 3 to 4 cloves garlic, minced
>
> ½ teaspoon hot red pepper flakes
>
> ½ cup white wine
>
> ½ cup fresh basil, chopped
>
> Sea salt

Shrimp

> 2 tablespoons olive oil
>
> 2 tablespoons (¼ stick) unsalted butter
>
> 2 cloves garlic, minced
>
> 2 pounds U-15 shrimp
>
> 2 bunches arugula, cleaned and chopped
>
> ½ cup grated Grana Padano cheese

1. Bring a large pot of salted water to a rapid boil, add the penne, and cook 8 to 10 minutes or until al dente, stirring occasionally. Drain and place in a serving bowl.

2. Meanwhile, prepare the sauce. Crush the tomatoes in a blender, using the pulse setting, until chunky. Blend on the liquefy setting until puréed and liquid. Set aside.

3. In a sauté pan heat the olive oil and butter over medium-high heat. Add the garlic and pepper flakes and sauté until the garlic is golden. Add the wine, basil, and reserved tomato purée and cook just to heat through, 5 to 6 minutes. Season with salt to taste. Pour the sauce over the penne and toss.

4. In another sauté pan, heat the olive oil and butter. Add the garlic and sauté for 2 to 3 minutes. Add the shrimp and sauté until they turn pink. Add the arugula and cook just until wilted. Stir to combine the ingredients and spoon over the penne. Top with the grated cheese and serve immediately.

Capricorn

December 22–January 19

FOOD TO BONE UP ON

These foods have been selected for Capricorn, ruler of the bones. Capricorns must eat foods that support the whole skeletal structure, including bones, joints, ligaments, and connective tissue so they can remain trim and fit as they are meant to be. That way they can put all their focus on being the powerful executives of the zodiac.

....

 Ruling Planet: Saturn
Body Part Ruled: Bones
House Ruled: Tenth, the house of social status, career
Element: Earth

Color: Brown
Stone: Garnet
Key Phrase: I use
Trait: Steadiness
Quality: Cardinal

Those born under the sign of Capricorn often find success in what they do—in particular, their careers. Capricorn rules the tenth house, the house of ambition and career. These Goats have the determination to succeed at anything they set their minds to. The tenth house is also the house of personal recognition and public status. Many Capricorns will attain a high degree of fame and many honors in their lifetime. They have a vision of what they want to accomplish, the stamina and fortitude to fulfill the goal, and the drive to push forward to the ultimate outcome.

When the sun moves through Capricorn, we celebrate two significant holidays, Christmas and New Year's. As we prepare on the thirty-first of December to wrap up the old year and embark on the new year, new resolutions, and new beginnings, the Capricorn reigns supreme. This sign, known for its tenacity and practicality, is associated with completing projects and setting new goals that appeal to their ambitious and disciplined nature.

Anyone looking to set their New Year's resolutions should defer to the Goat, whether it's to lose a few pounds (although they are rarely overweight), adhere to that new budget, or finally make a much-needed career change. All too many of us have lofty plans that often falter within days or even hours of the new year. No one can set a plan and stick to it like those Caps, as they are blessed with boundless patience and have been known to wait a lifetime for something they desire.

CAPRICORN IN THE KITCHEN

Capricorn natives are practical, ambitious, and have the tenacity and staying power to complete what they start long after the less disciplined would have ceded defeat. And that goes for their kitchens as well. They will undertake the most daunting of formal dinner parties and remain completely cool-headed under pressure that would send most running from the kitchen to the closest caterer.

They will use their over-the-top organizational skills to plan everything to the utmost detail. The menu will be straightforward, with soup, salad, entrée, and dessert courses. But this just means there won't be superfluous items among the elegant foods they have prepared.

Don't be surprised if your host or hostess has printed "formal attire" on your invitation, as they love putting on a tux or ball gown. And be sure to arrive on time, or the other guests may already be eating dinner. When you walk into the beautifully appointed living room, you will find cocktails waiting, but don't expect appetizers, as Capricorns don't want anything to take away from the meal.

Your host will greet you, share a toast, and usher you into the exquisite dining room. Once you are seated, the courses will be served in such perfect order, you may think there is a whole kitchen staff. But it is only the impeccable timing Capricorns possess that makes this possible. You will leave satiated with the feeling you just dined at the most prestigious restaurant.

CAPRICORN GUESTS

When inviting your Capricorn guests, remember that they are proper, formal, and serious in their acceptance of that invitation. They truly appreciate the formal dining table as it represents money and success. So set the table with beautiful creamy china with a silver or platinum border, rich navy blue damask napkins, and silver candelabra. Camellia or magnolia petals will give just the right touch.

But don't believe that Goats are stuffy and boring. They have a sense of humor and wit that may not be apparent at first. This wit, combined with a degree of flippancy, propels some Capricorns into the spotlights of stand-up comedy. Some of the world's great comedians are Capricorns. So if guests are starting to yawn at that dinner party, give the Goat a nudge and you may discover the next Jim Carrey.

Or if formal dinner parties aren't your cup of tea, to

appease the Capricorn's earthy nature, spread a quilt under a beautiful tree on a balmy day and have an impromptu picnic. Smell the aroma of freshly mown grass, rich brown earth, delicate flowers, and sumptuous foods and enjoy the day.

FEATURED CAPRICORN FOODS TO BONE UP ON

All these foods are great for Capricorn and the bones, but all signs will benefit from a strong skeletal structure.

Bananas. High in vitamin B_6 and potassium, bananas assist in the absorption of calcium, vital for healthy teeth and bones. Bananas are said to reduce stress and pain, especially leg cramps, which are a Capricorn ailment. Stress reduction can also benefit these overachievers, so maybe it shouldn't be "An apple a day keeps the doctor away," but a banana a day.

Bhutanese Red Rice. This beautiful red rice is high in antioxidants for healthy bones and powerful anti-inflammatory properties for arthritis protection. It has long been understood that the color is considered lucky in certain cultures, which would carry over to this grain. Like the custom of giving red envelopes on Chinese New Year to have luck with your finances, some are sure to have a special bowl of red rice on that day.

Cabbage. Cabbage is a good source of vitamin C and bursting with health benefits. It aids arthritis sufferers and has antiaging proponents. Many Capricorns look much younger in later life than their actual age, so if they consume cabbage throughout their lives they will appear extraordinarily youthful. This crucifer also promotes smooth, beautiful skin. Goats most certainly don't want Capricorn's scaly fishtail becoming unruly, so should indulge in cabbage dishes a few times a week. Any other signs with similar ailments may find the remedy in the cabbage patch.

Cloves. Cloves are anti-inflammatory and antibacterial and contain manganese. Dentists have long used clove extract to alleviate dental pain and further general oral health. These aspects make cloves an ideal spice for healthy Capricornian teeth and will reduce the inflammation of their arthritis. Cloves can also give support to all others and is a wonderful flavoring for many foods.

Molasses. Molasses is so high in calcium content that a spoonful a day can maintain proper calcium levels for healthy bones. It will also provide needed copper and manganese for support. For those Capricorns who sweeten their cereal and coffee, they should substitute molasses for their regular sweetener.

Pepitos. Pepitos, also called pumpkin seeds, are impressive in the aid to bone mineral density and arthritic distress due to content of zinc and their anti-inflammatory characteristics. They also are a good source of manganese and magnesium. These are a great snack for Caps to have on hand to enhance their strong bones and relieve any discomfort from arthritis.

Spinach. Spinach is very high in vitamin K, which contributes to bone health, and manganese, which lowers blood pressure. It also has anti-inflammatory properties. Capricorns are relatively even-tempered and this trait is enhanced by magical spinach. The Type-As of the zodiac could benefit from this stress reducer.

Tofu. Tofu is high in calcium and the isoflavones may deter the deterioration of bones caused by osteoporosis. It actually has as much, or more, calcium than milk. Tofu is especially beneficial to keep those Capricornian bones strong and healthy and their teeth pearly white.

*

Madelyn's Banana Bread

MAKES 2 LOAVES

This recipe was given to me by my friend Maureen. It was her mother Madelyn's recipe and it is literally the best banana bread I have ever had.

3 large eggs

6 ripe bananas, peeled and mashed

2 cups sugar

1 cup vegetable oil

2 teaspoons vanilla extract

3 cups all-purpose flour

1 teaspoon salt

3 teaspoons baking soda

2 teaspoons freshly grated nutmeg

2 teaspoons ground cinnamon

½ teaspoon ground cloves

1 cup chopped toasted walnuts

1. Preheat the oven to 325°F.

2. Spray two 9×5-inch loaf pans with nonstick cooking spray. Using an electric mixer, beat the eggs on medium-high speed for 2 minutes in a large mixing bowl. Add the bananas, sugar, oil, and vanilla and continue mixing until smooth.

3. In another mixing bowl, sift together the flour, salt, baking soda, nutmeg, cinnamon, and cloves. Mix the flour mixture into the banana mixture and stir until combined. Divide the batter between the two prepared loaf pans and bake the bread for 1 hour to 1 hour and 10 minutes until baked through in the center; a skewer inserted into the center of each loaf should come out clean.

Chicken and Napa Cabbage Egg Rolls with Ginger-Chili Vinaigrette

MAKES 12 EGG ROLLS

I promised Mary I would put these in the book! Here you go, Mary!

Egg Rolls

> 1 tablespoon vegetable oil
>
> 1 tablespoon sesame oil
>
> 2 teaspoons minced fresh garlic
>
> 2 teaspoons minced fresh ginger
>
> 1 boneless, skinless chicken breast, cooked and shredded
>
> 2 cups Napa cabbage, cut in thin chiffonade
>
> 1 cup julienned carrots
>
> 3 scallions, washed, trimmed, and sliced on the diagonal
>
> 8 shiitake mushrooms, stemmed and julienned
>
> ¼ cup store-bought vegetarian stir-fry sauce
>
> 12 egg roll wrappers
>
> 1 egg, beaten

Vinaigrette

> ½ cup seasoned rice vinegar
>
> ½ cup low-sodium soy sauce
>
> ½ teaspoon chili oil
>
> 2 cups vegetable oil

1. Heat the vegetable and sesame oils in a wok over medium-high heat. Add 1 teaspoon of the garlic and 1 teaspoon of the ginger and stir constantly for 1 minute. Add the chicken and stir for another minute. Add the cabbage, carrots, scallions, and mushrooms and stir-fry for 3 minutes. Add the stir-fry sauce and cook for 1 minute until the vegetables and sauce are combined. Remove from the heat and transfer to a baking sheet and let cool. Drain off any excess liquid.

2. In a small bowl, whisk together the rice vinegar, soy sauce, the remaining ginger and garlic, and the chili oil. Pour into a small serving bowl.

3. Measure ¼ cup of the vegetable-chicken mixture in a measuring cup and place in the center of one egg roll wrapper. Cover the remaining wrappers with a damp cloth while rolling the egg rolls to keep them from drying out. Fold two corners of the wrapper together in the middle and roll tightly and, using a pastry brush, moisten the edges with the egg wash to seal the roll. If you are just learning to wrap, be sure to have extra wrappers on hand in case they tear.

4. Heat the vegetable oil to 375°F in a wok or deep fryer. Line a baking sheet with paper towels and set aside. Fry the egg rolls until golden brown. Remove from the oil with a stainless steel skimmer and transfer to the lined baking sheet. Serve the egg rolls hot with the ginger-chili vinaigrette.

✳

Roasted Pork Tenderloin with Glazed Apples and Cloves

SERVES 4

My husband loves this dish, so this one's for you, honey!

   2 teaspoons minced fresh ginger

   1 teaspoon minced fresh garlic

   ½ cup hoisin sauce

   2 tablespoons low-sodium soy sauce

   2 tablespoons dry sherry

   ¼ cup olive oil

   One 1½-pound pork tenderloin

   2 tablespoons (¼ stick) unsalted butter

   2 Granny Smith apples, cored, peeled, and thinly sliced

   ½ cup apple cider

   ¼ cup Calvados

   6 whole cloves

   ½ teaspoon salt

1. Mix together the ginger, garlic, hoisin, soy sauce, sherry, and olive oil in a small bowl. Pour the marinade over the pork tenderloin in a shallow dish, cover, and refrigerate overnight.

2. Preheat the oven to 350°F. Transfer the tenderloin to a roasting pan. Roast for 25 to 30 minutes until the internal temperature registers 160°F. Remove from the oven and let rest for 10 minutes.

3. Melt the butter in a medium saucepan. Add the apples and cook for 5 minutes. Pour in the apple cider, Calvados, cloves, and salt. Bring to a boil, reduce the heat, and simmer for 20 minutes. Remove and discard the cloves.

4. Slice the pork tenderloin into medallions. Arrange the medallions on serving plates and spoon the apples and sauce over the top. Serve immediately.

Molasses Cookies

MAKES 5 DOZEN COOKIES

My mom used to make these for us when we were kids and this recipe has been passed down to my daughter.

    16 tablespoons (2 sticks) unsalted butter
    1 cup granulated sugar
    ½ cup firmly packed light brown sugar
    2 large eggs, beaten
    ¼ cup molasses
    2 ¼ cups all-purpose flour
    2 teaspoons baking soda
    ½ teaspoon salt
    1 teaspoon ground cinnamon
    1 teaspoon ground ginger
    ½ teaspoon ground cloves

1. Preheat the oven to 350°F.

2. In the bowl of an electric mixer, cream the butter with ½ cup of the granulated sugar and the brown sugar on medium-high speed. Reduce the speed to medium and add the eggs one at a time. Add the molasses and continue to mix. Remove the bowl from the mixer and set aside. In a mixing bowl, sift together all the dry ingredients except for the remaining ½ cup of granulated sugar. Stir the dry mixture into the butter mixture until completely blended. Cover the dough with plastic wrap and refrigerate for at least 1 hour.

3. Using a tablespoon-size ice cream scoop, scoop the dough and roll it into balls. Roll the balls in the remaining granulated sugar. Place the balls onto a greased baking sheet, spacing them 2 inches apart, and bake for 8 to 10 minutes. Remove from the oven and transfer to wire racks to cool.

Pumpkin-Bran Muffins with Pepito Seeds

MAKES 12 MUFFINS

This is my mom's recipe she made for me while I was pregnant with my daughter. She knew I loved pumpkin and needed lots of fiber.

2 large eggs

¾ cup firmly packed brown sugar

1 cup mashed pumpkin

1 cup buttermilk

¼ cup vegetable oil

1 teaspoon pure vanilla extract

1 cup whole wheat pastry flour

¾ cup all-purpose flour

1 cup unprocessed wheat bran

1½ teaspoons baking powder

½ teaspoon baking soda

1 teaspoon ground cinnamon

½ teaspoon freshly grated nutmeg

Pinch of ground cloves

½ teaspoon salt

½ cup pepito seeds

1. Preheat the oven to 375°F.

2. Line a standard 12-well muffin pan with paper liners. Whisk the eggs and brown sugar together in a medium bowl until smooth. Whisk in the mashed pumpkin, buttermilk, and vanilla.

3. In a medium bowl, combine all the dry ingredients except the pepito seeds. Add the dry ingredients to the pumpkin mixture and stir until blended. Divide the batter among the 12 wells and sprinkle with the pepito seeds. Bake for 15 to 20 minutes until a toothpick inserted into the center of a muffin comes out clean. Transfer the muffins to a wire rack and cool for 10 minutes.

Spinach and Feta Frittata

SERVES 12

This is a family favorite. We have this several times a year for brunch.

   1 loaf Pugliese bread, cut into ¼-inch slices

   2 cups shredded mozzarella cheese

   1 tablespoon olive oil

   1 tablespoon unsalted butter

   1 onion, cut into medium dice

   1 red bell pepper, seeds and membranes removed, diced

   1 pound frozen chopped spinach, thawed and drained

   ½ pound mushrooms, stemmed and sliced

   2 teaspoons dried oregano

   1 teaspoon salt

   Freshly ground black pepper

   8 ounces French feta cheese, crumbled

   18 large eggs, beaten

   2 cups half-and-half

1. Preheat the oven to 375°F.

2. Spray a 12 × 10 × 4-inch pan with nonstick cooking spray. Line the bottom of the pan with the bread, so it is completely covered. Sprinkle the shredded cheese over the bread.

3. In a large skillet, heat the oil and butter over medium-high heat. Add the onion and bell pepper and sauté until tender. Add the spinach and mushrooms, stirring constantly until tender. Add the oregano, salt, and pepper and continue to cook for 2 minutes. Remove the pan from the heat and transfer the vegetables to a colander to drain. Squeeze the liquid out of the vegetables. Sprinkle the vegetables over the cheese and the feta over the vegetables.

4. Whisk together the eggs and half-and-half. Pour the mixture evenly over the vegetables in the dish. Bake the frittata for 1 hour to 1 hour and 15 minutes until golden brown and the egg is cooked through. Remove from the oven and let cool for 15 minutes before cutting and serving.

Garlicky Tofu Stir-Fry

SERVES 6

Serve this with the Bhutanese Rice (recipe follows).

½ teaspoon minced fresh ginger

½ teaspoon plus 1 tablespoon minced fresh garlic

¼ cup low-sodium soy sauce

2 tablespoons sesame oil

1 pound extra-firm tofu, cut into small cubes

1 tablespoon olive oil

1 yellow onion, medium diced

2 cups sugar snap peas

2 carrots, peeled, halved, and cut on the diagonal

1 cup enoki mushrooms

2 tablespoons black bean sauce

2 tablespoons sherry

1 tablespoon brown sugar

Cooked rice for serving

1. In a small bowl, whisk together the ginger, ½ teaspoon of garlic, soy sauce, and 1 tablespoon of the sesame oil. Add the tofu, cover, and refrigerate overnight.

2. Preheat the oven to 350°F. Spray a baking sheet with nonstick cooking spray. Drain the tofu of the marinade and spread it evenly on the prepared pan. Bake for 30 minutes.

3. Heat the olive oil and the remaining 1 tablespoon of sesame oil in a wok over medium-high heat. Add the garlic and onions and stir-fry constantly for 2 minutes. Add the peas and carrots and continue stir-frying for 3 minutes. Add the mushrooms and stir-fry for 2 minutes. Add the black bean sauce, sherry, and brown sugar and stir-fry until the vegetables are coated. Add the tofu and mix gently together, remove from the heat, and serve immediately with rice.

✳

Bhutanese Rice (Red Rice)

SERVES 6

If you've never tried this, it's a must. So nutty and delicious!

> One 15-ounce bag Bhutanese rice, rinsed
> 2¾ cups chicken stock
> ¼ cup dry sherry
> 1 cup scallions, sliced
> 2 tablespoons (¼ stick) unsalted butter
> ½ teaspoon salt

1. Bring the chicken stock, sherry, scallions, butter, and salt to a boil in a medium pot.
2. Add the rice, reduce the heat, cover, and simmer for 20 minutes. Fluff the rice with a fork and serve immediately.

Aquarius

January 20–February 18

CONTROL-THE-FLOW FOODS

All these foods have been carefully selected for Aquarius, as this sign rules the circulatory system. Aquarius is the intellectual of the zodiac, and like some of the most intelligent people in the world, can be quite eccentric. You can probably recognize an Aquarian right off the bat, for instance your genius college professor whose head is so in the clouds he doesn't realize he has on two different shoes. Yes, he most likely is an Aquarius!

. . . .

Symbol: The Water Bearer
Ruling Planet: Uranus
Body Part Ruled: Circulatory system
House Ruled: Eleventh, the house
 of friends, acquaintances,
 detached relationships, societies

Element: Air
Color: Bright blue
Stone: Amethyst
Key Phrase: I know
Trait: Friendliness
Quality: Fixed

Aquarius and its ruling planet Uranus rule the eleventh house of social networking and all your acquaintances. And social they are; Aquarians have been called the zodiac's friendliest sign. Their friends are an eclectic group, consisting of intellectuals, artists, conservatives, and social rebels. The Aquarians are not confined or defined by this group; they consider themselves to be free thinkers, respect idiosyncrasies of others, and above all desire their own freedom.

With an artistic flair, particularly in music and drama, many Aquarians pursue the acting profession. Inventive and original, they can take a role to the limit more so than other signs. With their natural communication skills and brilliant minds, the Aquarius actor is quite eloquent.

Aquarius is an air sign, but is called the Water Bearer—an unusual dichotomy. But unusual could be a keyword for Aquarius. They're drawn to the unusual in all things, places, individuals, and work. Often viewed as eccentric, avant-garde, or bohemian, some Aquarians go so far as to adopt an unusual style, opting for the hippie or New Age look. But since we are in the Age of Aquarius, what more appropriate sign could take up that standard than these unique creatures.

Aquarians are scientific, altruistic, intelligent, and very humanitarian. They are focused, detached, and their thinking has a futuristic quality fused with genius. Aquarians are often seen as the absentminded professor, eccentric and brilliant, but so distracted they forget their own basic needs, such as food.

AQUARIUS IN THE KITCHEN

And speaking of food, you have to know that if your Aquarian friend *ever* says he wants to have a dinner party, you *must* volunteer to help. Or maybe you should just take charge. You can follow him around, get his ideas about the date, menu, guest list, and pull his address book off his computer. And then you're on your own. Well, not exactly, he will gladly pay for everything!

This is not to say that Aquarius doesn't want to entertain and serve a wonderful meal to his wide group of friends. It's just that he can't seem to focus on all those pesky details long enough to make it happen on his own. He will be most grateful for all your hard work, appreciate the delicious meal you prepared, and delight at how you brought his vision to fruition. Just be sure to remind him what time dinner is!

AQUARIUS GUESTS

Lovers of social occasions, your Aquarian friends will quickly accept an invitation to dinner. Although they have their favorite dishes, the Aquarius native will welcome any meal as he often forgets to eat altogether. Aquarians abhor public displays of affection; don't seat them next to the gushy, touchy-feely type or invite them to a romantic candlelight soiree. Although Valentine's Day is ruled by Aquarius, the Water Bearer prefers any romantic occasion to be private.

They relish conversations that stimulate their minds. So be sure to include at least one other intellectual on your guest list to converse with the Water Bearers. The perfect evening for Aquarius would be a stargazing party. Set up a telescope and view the constellations with an astronomer guide that can point out the seven stars that form the "Winter Hexagon." The seven stars are Sirius, Capella, Aldebaran, Rigel, Procyon, Pollux, and Castor, from six constellations, which, of course, your Aquarius guest will already know.

Begin by serving cocktails with hors d'oeuvres that you call Galactic Martinis and Orion Canapés, and end with Milky Way Brownies. Set up a hundred clear glass votive candleholders with tea lights for a dazzling display. Use strings of white Christmas lights to light the room and patio, and play the soundtrack from *2001: A Space Odyssey*. Your Aquarian friend will be over the moon.

FEATURED AQUARIUS CONTROL-THE-FLOW FOODS

All these foods are great for Aquarius and the circulatory system, but all signs will benefit from the blood-circulating properties.

Blueberries. These great little berries have been deemed one of the superfruits of all time. They have powerful antioxidant properties that work miracles for the circulatory system, controlling the proper blood flow through the vessels and the amount of oxygen in the blood, and providing protection against disease. In ancient times blueberries were worn in pouches to ward off evil—better that Water Bearers eat them for protection against circulatory evils.

Carrots. Beta carotene, the master antioxidant, is prevalent in carrots and it benefits the circulatory system by lowering blood pressure and cholesterol. If bunnies are smart enough to eat their fill of carrots, surely Aquarians, the absentminded professor types of the zodiac, can use their mega-intelligence to do the same thing. All signs wishing to gain these benefits should follow a bunny to the carrot patch.

Cayenne. Cayenne is the ultimate spice for the circulatory system, from the tiny cells of capillaries to the large arteries and veins pumping our blood throughout the body. It regulates blood pressure, eliminates bad cholesterol, and can actually cleanse the blood vessels. Aquarians should have cayenne readily at hand in their pantry, not that they will really cook, but to add to whatever quick meal they picked up on the way home.

Chicken. Chicken is a good protein source for Aquarius as it contains trace amounts of selenium that support blood cells. It is also very high in tryptophan, the essential amino acid that makes you sleepy, another good reason for the Water Bearer to make it their poultry of choice. The overactive Aquarius mind has to rest sometime, even if it's a few quick winks after their chicken sandwich lunch.

Hearts of Palm. High in iron, potassium, folate, fiber, manganese, magnesium, and the antioxidant vitamin C, hearts of palm help the flow of blood and the circulation of oxygen. They are also very unusual, which appeals to the eccentric nature of the Aquarian. The Water Bearer host or hostess would delight in serving a strategically placed pile of hearts of palm, the more bizarre the better.

Okinawan Sweet Potatoes. This Japanese strain of sweet potato is loaded with vitamin A, iron, and manganese, all beneficial for a healthy circulatory system. These properties help reduce cholesterol and fat, support oxygen in the blood, and reduce inflammation causing those pesky afflictions, gout and edema, which can plague Aquarian natives. These purple tubers may seem unusual, but that is perfect for Aquarius, as they love all unusual things.

Pistachio Nuts. Pistachio nuts are high in antioxidants, vitamins A and D, potassium, and phosphorus, and are known to lower cholesterol, all of which offer wonderful support for a healthy circulatory system. They are the perfect snack for the cerebral Aquarius native to have on hand for those times they forget to eat.

Sea Bass. Sea bass is high in omega-3 fatty acids, which balance the intake of omega-6 fatty acids. Omega-6s are so prevalent in vegetables and abundant in other foods that many tend to overindulge, resulting in inflammation diseases, such as gout and edema, both Aquarius ailments. The Aquarian native will benefit from regular doses of omega-6s, so they need to make regular trips to their local fishmonger.

*

Miso-Marinated Pan-Seared Sea Bass

SERVES 4

This is a local island favorite! If you like miso-glazed cod, you will love this, too!

Fish

> Four 6-ounce sea bass fillets
>
> 2 tablespoons olive oil

Marinade

> ¼ cup sake
>
> ¼ cup mirin
>
> 2 tablespoons white miso
>
> 1 teaspoon sesame oil
>
> 1 tablespoon low-sodium soy sauce
>
> 2 tablespoons brown sugar
>
> 1 scallion, sliced
>
> 2 garlic cloves, minced
>
> ½ teaspoon peeled and finely minced fresh ginger

1. Preheat the oven to 300°F. Place the sea bass fillets in a large ziplock bag. Mix all the ingredients for the marinade together in a small bowl. Pour the marinade over the fish, close the bag securely, and place in the refrigerator for up to 6 hours.

2. Add the olive oil to an oven-proof sauté pan over medium-high heat until it begins to smoke slightly. Add the fish to the pan, skin side down, and sear for 5 minutes, or until the skin is crisp and golden. Turn and sear on the opposite side until golden. Transfer to the oven for 10 minutes. Remove the fish from the oven and serve immediately.

✳

Blueberry Muffins with Lemon Curd

SERVES 12

Blueberries and lemon! Heaven!

> 2 cups all-purpose flour
>
> 1 teaspoon baking powder
>
> ½ teaspoon salt
>
> 8 tablespoons (1 stick) unsalted butter, softened to room temperature
>
> 1 cup sugar
>
> 2 large eggs
>
> 1 teaspoon pure vanilla extract
>
> ¼ cup sour cream
>
> ¼ cup milk
>
> 1 tablespoon finely grated lemon zest
>
> 1 ½ cups blueberries
>
> 4 tablespoons lemon curd

1. Preheat the oven to 375°F.

2. In a bowl, mix together the sifted flour, baking powder, and salt. Set aside.

3. In the bowl of an electric mixer, cream the butter and sugar on medium speed until fluffy. Add the eggs one at a time and beat until incorporated. Add the vanilla, sour cream, milk, and lemon zest and mix well. Add the dry ingredients and stir until fully incorporated. Fold in the blueberries.

4. Line a standard 12-well muffin pan with paper liners. Fill each well half-full with batter. Put 1 teaspoon of lemon curd in the center and top with the remaining batter. Bake 20 to 25 minutes until golden.

Creamy Coconut-Carrot Soup

SERVES 8

If you have little children, this is a great way to get them to eat their carrots. I used to put this in a mug for my daughter and she always came back for more.

1 large onion, chopped

3 celery stalks, chopped

3 leeks, white part only, trimmed, thoroughly cleaned,
    sliced

1 tablespoon fresh minced ginger

1 tablespoon olive oil

2 pounds baby carrots

3 lemongrass stalks, trimmed, slit lengthwise and opened up

6 cups chicken broth

12 ounces frozen coconut milk, thawed

Salt and freshly ground black pepper

Crème fraîche for garnish

1. In large pot, sweat the onions, celery, leeks, and ginger over medium heat for 5 minutes. Add carrots, lemongrass, and chicken stock. Bring to a boil, reduce the heat, and simmer 20 minutes, or until the carrots are tender. Remove the pot from the heat and remove and discard the lemongrass. Add the coconut milk and allow the soup to cool slightly.

2. Transfer the soup to a blender and blend until creamy, working in batches. Return the soup to the pot, reheat, and season to taste with salt and pepper. Ladle into bowls and swirl crème fraîche on top. Serve immediately.

* * *

Spicy (Cayenne) Cocktail Nut Mix

MAKES 8 CUPS NUT MIX

These will spice up your cocktail party!

> 8 tablespoons (1 stick) unsalted butter
>
> ¾ cup firmly packed brown sugar
>
> 1 tablespoon Worcestershire Sauce
>
> 2 teaspoons garlic powder
>
> ¼ teaspoon cayenne pepper
>
> 1 teaspoon ground cumin
>
> 1 teaspoon ground coriander
>
> 1 tablespoon sea salt
>
> 2 cups whole almonds
>
> 2 cups cashews
>
> 2 cups pecans
>
> 2 cups walnuts

1. Preheat the oven to 250°F.

2. In a heavy-bottomed pan, mix together the butter, brown sugar, and Worcestershire. Add the garlic powder, cayenne, cumin, coriander, and sea salt and mix to combine. Add the nuts and stir to coat.

3. Transfer the nut mix to a baking sheet sprayed with non-stick cooking spray and spread out in a single layer. Bake for 30 to 40 minutes, or until browned.

✳

Chicken Katsu

SERVES 4

This is the Japanese version of your grandmother's fried chicken! You won't even miss the skin with the panko crust.

Katzu Sauce

> ½ cup ketchup
>
> 2 tablespoons Worcestershire sauce
>
> 2 tablespoons sugar
>
> 2 tablespoons tamari
>
> 2 tablespoons mirin
>
> 2 tablespoons sake
>
> 2 garlic cloves, finely minced
>
> 2 teaspoons peeled, finely minced ginger
>
> 1 scallion, white part only, finely minced

Chicken

  4 boneless, skinless chicken breasts, halved

  1 cup all-purpose flour

  Salt and freshly ground black pepper

  4 large eggs

  1 cup panko bread crumbs

  2 cups vegetable oil

1. Combine all the ingredients for the sauce in a saucepan and bring to a boil. Reduce the heat and simmer until thickened, about 10 minutes. Remove from the heat, but keep warm.

2. Preheat the oven to 300°F.

3. Place the chicken in a large ziplock bag and seal. Place the bag on a cutting board and pound with a mallet until the chicken is ¼ inch thick.

4. In a bowl, mix together the flour, salt, and pepper. In another bowl, beat the eggs. Put the panko crumbs in a third bowl. Dredge the chicken pieces in the seasoned flour, shaking off the excess. Dip each piece into the beaten eggs, and then dredge in the panko.

5. Line a baking sheet with paper towels. Heat 1 cup of the vegetable oil in a heavy-bottomed pot. Add the chicken pieces, a few at a time, and cook until golden, turning once. Transfer pieces to the prepared baking sheet to drain excess oil. Spray another baking sheet with nonstick spray. Transfer chicken to sprayed sheet and place in the oven to keep warm. Continue until all the chicken is cooked. Place the chicken on serving plates and serve with warm sauce.

＊

Smoked Molokai Sweet Potatoes
SERVES 8

I love the purple color of Molokai or Okinawan sweet potatoes. But if they are unavailable in your area, this recipe works equally well with sweet potatoes.

> 3 pounds Molokai or Okinawan sweet potatoes, peeled and
>   quartered
> 4 tablespoons (½ stick) unsalted butter
> ¾ cup heavy cream
> 1 teaspoon liquid smoke or to taste
> Salt and freshly ground black pepper

1. Bring a large pot of water to a boil. Add the potatoes and cook until tender, about 30 minutes. Drain.
2. Add the butter and liquid smoke to the potatoes and, using an electric mixer, blend the potatoes on low speed. Gradually add the cream and whip until the potatoes are creamy. Season with salt and pepper to taste. Transfer the potatoes to a serving bowl.

✳

Chopped Hearts of Palm with Blue Cheese Dressing and Bacon

SERVES 6

This is a nice salad to serve to the ladies for lunch.

Blue Cheese Dressing

> 6 ounces blue cheese, crumbled
>
> ½ cup mayonnaise
>
> ½ cup buttermilk
>
> 1 tablespoon lemon juice
>
> 1 ½ tablespoons peeled and finely minced shallots
>
> 1 garlic clove, finely minced
>
> Salt and freshly ground black pepper

Salad

> One 15-ounce jar hearts of palm, drained and rinsed
>
> 2 hearts of romaine lettuce
>
> 1 tomato, seeded and cut into small dice
>
> 6 to 8 slices bacon, cooked until crisp and crumbled
>
> 4 hard-boiled eggs, finely chopped

1. In a bowl, mash the blue cheese with a fork. Add the shallots, garlic, and lemon juice, and mix well. Whisk in the mayonnaise and buttermilk. Season with salt and pepper to taste.

2. Put the hearts of palm in a bowl and pour over the dressing. Cover and refrigerate for 24 hours.

3. Chop the romaine, place in a large salad bowl, and toss with the tomatoes. Remove the hearts of palm from the bowl, reserving the dressing, and place on a cutting board. Chop into ½-inch pieces and add to the salad bowl along with dressing and toss well. Portion equally among six serving plates; garnish with the bacon and chopped egg.

✳

Pistachio Mousse Tarts

SERVES 6

This mousse is to die for, with just the right creaminess and crunch!

> Six 6-inch tart shells (purchased or homemade)
> 6 ounces semisweet chocolate, chopped
> 1 cup heavy cream
> 1 cup confectioners' sugar
> 2 teaspoons pistachio extract
> 8 ounces mascarpone cheese
> 1 cup ground pistachios

1. In a double boiler, melt the chocolate. Using a pastry brush, brush the melted chocolate on the sides and bottoms of the tart shells to the desired thickness. Place in the refrigerator to set.

2. In the bowl of an electric mixer, whip the heavy cream until soft peaks begin to form. Add the sugar and the pistachio extract and continue whipping the cream until stiff peaks are formed.

3. In a separate bowl, beat the mascarpone cheese until fluffy. Fold the whipped cream into the mascarpone. Fold in the pistachios.

4. Transfer the mixture to a ziplock bag and seal tightly. Snip off one corner of the bag to make a pastry bag. Remove the tart shells from the refrigerator and pipe the mousse into each shell. Refrigerate the filled shells for 2 to 4 hours, or until well set.

12

Pisces

February 19–March 20

IMMUNE-BOOSTING FOODS

All these foods have been carefully selected for Pisces, as this sign rules the immune system. Pisces is the mystic of the zodiac, full of sympathy for all the world's creatures. They are empathetic and sometimes take on the problems of those around them as if to remove the pain and suffering of the world. This can cause wear and tear on immunity, so Pisces, and any other sign, can bolster their immune systems with these great foods.

....

Symbol: Two fish
Ruling Planet: Neptune
Body Part Ruled: Immune system
House Ruled: Twelfth, the house of endings, collective unconscious, secrets, spirituality

Element: Water
Color: Sea green
Stone: Aquamarine
Key Phrase: I believe
Trait: Compassion
Quality: Mutable

Pisces and its ruler Neptune rule the twelfth house of spirituality, the unconscious, and hidden secrets. This mystical sign has a foot in both worlds, the material and the divine (spiritual), and as a result they can be dreamers, never quite fully engaged in their human existence. But this also makes them compassionate and sensitive. Pisces natives are more intuitive and psychic than any other sign and they use this ability to communicate, not only with those around them on the earthly plane, but also with those from the illusionary realm.

While it may sound as if Pisces may not be quite in touch with reality, boarding on delusional, this isn't true. Illusion and phenomena allude to seeing things that aren't there, things that are scary or go bump in the night. But just because "normal" eyes can't see something doesn't mean it isn't there or that it comes from the realm of darkness. Just as a blind man's other senses are heightened and he "sees," Pisces natives have the eyes to see what other signs do not, psychic eyes, piercing the veil between the heavens and earth.

As long as they keep one foot on the ground they will remain true to that inner voice, able to inspire others without losing themselves. This is their true joy.

PISCES IN THE KITCHEN

The Pisces host will bring an otherworldly approach to their dinner parties. They are the pleasure seekers of the zodiac who will draw felicity from their relationship with food. Pisces have a sense of adventure when it comes to their kitchen as they utilize all their creativity and artistic flair to please their guests, as well as their own inner well-being. There is no other way Pisces natives would rather show their appreciation for their friends.

You can expect the food your Pisces host or hostess prepares to warm the cockles of your heart and have an ethereal quality, unlike anything you have ever experienced. The event will be surrounded with mystique and illusion. Don't be surprised if the evening is topped off with special entertainment—an illusionist pulling magical trinkets out of the air before disappearing in a puff of smoke!

PISCES GUESTS

Your Pisces friends are superb guests if you can get them out of the clouds, which shouldn't be too difficult if you promise them a meal of something from the sea, such as fresh cracked crab. They adore all swimming entrées, not literally swimming when served, but that have previously resided below the water's surface! Pisces have the ability to inspire those around them to excellence just by being in the Piscean presence. So having one or two Fish on your guest list will be the combination of a personal growth seminar by osmosis and a grand dinner party all in one.

Being a water sign gives credence to the fact that Pisces natives adore pale sea green. If you happen to have elegant dinnerware in this shade hidden away in your china cabinet, be sure to use it. If not, don't be concerned; just use table linens in varying shades of this soothing color. Exotic flowers, especially water lilies, floating in crystal bowls add the finishing touch to a beautiful table.

Sights, aromas, and sounds, all things that can assail the senses, are most appealing to and appreciated by Pisces. Enhance the colors of the entrée with garnishes of bright yellow lemons, bright green parsley, and colorful spices. While others may turn up their noses at the scent of crab or other seafood wafting through the dining room, Pisces will think they have died and gone to heaven. Play soothing classical music such as the CD *Pachelbel Canon with Ocean Sounds* and your Piscean guests may never want to leave.

FEATURED PISCES IMMUNE-BOOSTING FOODS

All these foods are great for Pisces and the immune system, but all signs will benefit from the immunity-building properties.

Chipotle Peppers (smoked jalapeños). The capsaicin in chipotle peppers has properties that stimulate and boost the immune system. They are loaded with vitamins A and C and are antimicrobial, which also improves immunity and helps the body fight infection. Pisces natives should keep a supply of chipotle peppers on hand, or order authentic Mexican dishes containing these great peppers a couple times a week to keep away the cold bugs.

Corn. The phytonutrients in corn are instrumental for establishing a strong immune system and rebuilding cells harmed by free radicals. They contain loads of vitamin C that adds further protection for immunity. Eating corn a few times a week will benefit Pisces natives. Grilled corn on the cob is one sure way to make a Pisces happy, especially if it is served alongside some grilled sea creature to appease their love of things from the ocean.

Crab. High in zinc and selenium, the trace mineral that works hand in hand with vitamin E, crab functions as an antioxidant to support the immune system. This is doubly important for Pisces natives because not only are they prone to viral infections that attack immunity, but they are equally prone to foot injuries, which can turn into nasty sores. You can't have anything that prevents Pisceans from keeping at least one of those tootsies on the ground, so crab should work wonders in both areas.

Cumin. High in vitamins A and C and iron, cumin is a definite cold-buster and supports the Pisces immune system. Cumin naturally disinfects and protects the body with its big supply of essential oils. It is one of the most widely used spices in India, which is a very mystical, spiritual country. Cumin is the perfect spice for this spiritual sign to ward off any attacks to their immunity.

Greek Yogurt. Greek yogurt contains probiotics, the good bacteria that aids the body in disease prevention. Eating yogurt every day is possibly one of the best immune system enhancements for eradicating bugs and germs to keep the Pisces system disease free, plus it has more protein than any other yogurt. Since these natives can have their heads in the clouds more often than not, they can be oblivious until one of these invaders has taken hold. All other signs should take a clue from Pisces and learn to like yogurt.

Lamb. A 3-ounce portion of lamb contains zinc, selenium, vitamins B_3 and B_{12}, and omega-3 fatty acids, as well as protein. Zinc and selenium are excellent immunity benefits. Also high in tryptophan, which makes us sleepy, lamb can be just what Pisces needs to assure getting the rest that allows the immune system's recovery. B vitamins provide energy for exercise, which will also help Pisces keep those nasty viruses at bay.

Maple Syrup. This natural sweetener is high in zinc, manganese, and antioxidants, which protect the immune system by supporting the white blood cells. It is perfect for Pisces and any of the other signs who may have compromised immunity. They should all switch to maple syrup for those times when sweetener is needed.

Oats. High in manganese, oats boost immunity strength and rev up the body's infection response. Their antioxidant properties are an added bonus for Pisces. Oats are a healthy breakfast suggestion for all signs. But when Pisces top off their oatmeal with a couple teaspoons of maple syrup, they gain double protection from all those flu bugs waiting to attack.

*

Zesty Chile-Cheese Cornbread

I make this with my chili but it is good on its own right out of the pan!

SERVES 12

1 ½ cups cornmeal

1 ½ cups all-purpose flour

1 teaspoon baking soda

2 teaspoons baking powder

2 tablespoons sugar

2 teaspoons salt

3 large eggs

2 cups buttermilk

½ cup canola oil

1 cup shredded Colby-Jack cheese

One 4-ounce can diced green chiles

1 cup thawed white corn, drained

1. Preheat the oven to 375°F.

2. Spray a 13 × 9 × 2-inch baking pan with nonstick cooking spray. In a medium bowl, mix together all the sifted dry ingredients.

3. In another bowl, beat together the eggs, buttermilk, and canola oil. Add the dry ingredients to the wet mixture and combine. Add the cheese, chiles, and white corn and stir to incorporate. Spread the batter out evenly in the prepared baking pan. Bake for 30 to 35 minutes, or until golden brown.

✳

Crab Cakes with Julienned Mango and Red Pepper Aioli

SERVES 4

I've put a twist on the crab cake with the lemongrass! It is so fragrant and is so complementary!

Crab Cakes

 2 tablespoons olive oil

 ¼ cup minced shallots

 ½ cup red bell pepper, seeds and membranes removed, cut
  into very small dice

 1 celery stalk, cut into very small dice

 1 tablespoon minced lemongrass

 1 pound crabmeat, cleaned and picked over for shells

 3 cups panko bread crumbs

 ¼ cup mayonnaise

 1 large egg, beaten

 Juice of 1 lemon

 ¼ cup chopped cilantro

 Salt and freshly ground black pepper

Aioli

> 2 tablespoons olive oil
>
> 1 teaspoon minced garlic
>
> 1 roasted red bell pepper, cut into pieces
>
> ½ cup fresh basil leaves
>
> 1 cup mayonnaise
>
> 2 cups vegetable oil
>
> 1 mango, peeled, pitted, and julienned for garnish

1. In a sauté pan, heat 2 tablespoons of the olive oil over medium-high heat. Add the shallots, bell pepper, celery, and lemongrass and sauté for 5 minutes, or until the vegetables are tender. Remove from heat and let cool.

2. In a large bowl, mix together the crabmeat, 1 cup of the panko, the mayonnaise, the egg, 1 tablespoon of the lemon juice, and the cilantro. Add the cooled vegetables and incorporate into the crab mixture. Season with salt and pepper to taste. Roll the crab into balls the size of a golf ball. Roll the balls in the remaining panko bread crumbs. Line up in a container, cover, and put in the freezer for 30 minutes.

3. Meanwhile, prepare the aioli and garnish. In a sauté pan, heat the 2 tablespoons olive oil over medium-high heat. Add the garlic and sauté for 1 minute. Add the roasted bell pepper and basil and sauté together for another minute. Remove from the heat and let cool.

4. In the bowl of a food processor, mix the remaining 1 cup of mayonnaise, the remaining lemon juice, and the roasted bell pepper mixture. Pulse until you reach a smooth consistency. Transfer the aioli from the food processor to a small bowl, cover, and refrigerate.

5. Preheat the oven to 300°F.

6. Line a baking pan with paper towels. Form the balls into patties; the balls will be really easy to work with when removed from the freezer. In a large skillet, heat the vegetable oil over medium heat. When the oil is hot, fry the crab cakes until golden brown on each side, about 5 minutes.

7. Transfer the crab cakes to the lined baking sheet to absorb the excess oil, then transfer to another pan and keep warm in the oven until all the crab cakes have been cooked. Serve the crab cakes with the red pepper aioli spooned over the top and garnish with the julienned mango.

✳

Herb-Crusted Leg of Lamb

SERVES 8

Serve this with Tzatziki Sauce and the Roasted Potatoes and Cipollini Onions with Cumin (recipes follow).

> One 5- to 6-pound boneless leg of lamb
> ½ cup fresh garlic cloves

½ cup fresh rosemary leaves

½ cup fresh thyme leaves

¼ cup freshly squeezed lemon juice

½ cup olive oil

1 tablespoon kosher salt

2 teaspoons freshly ground black pepper

1. Add the garlic, rosemary, thyme, lemon juice, olive oil, salt, and pepper to the bowl of a food processor. Pulse until the mixture has a paste-like consistency. Transfer from the food processor to a small bowl. Rub the paste over the lamb so it is thoroughly coated with the paste. Cover and refrigerate for 24 hours.

2. Preheat the oven to 450°F.

3. Place the lamb on a roasting rack inside a roasting pan. Roast the lamb for 20 minutes, then reduce the heat to 325°F and continue roasting for another hour, or until the internal temperature of the meat is 135°F. Transfer the lamb rack from the roasting pan to a cutting board. Let rest for 15 minutes before carving. Serve with *Tzatziki Sauce* (recipe on page 235).

✳

Roasted Potatoes and Cipollini Onions with Cumin

SERVES 8

A great combination of flavors!

> 3 pounds fingerling potatoes, quartered
> 1 pound cipollini onions, cut into half-moons
> 4 tablespoons olive oil
> 1 tablespoon ground cumin
> ¼ cup chopped fresh oregano
> 1 tablespoon chopped fresh thyme
> Kosher salt
> Freshly ground black pepper

1. Preheat the oven to 400°F. Spray a rimmed baking sheet with nonstick cooking spray.

2. In a large mixing bowl, toss together the potatoes, onions, olive oil, cumin, oregano, and thyme. Season with salt and pepper to taste. Spread out the potatoes and onions evenly on the prepared baking sheet and roast in the oven for 50 to 60 minutes, or until the potatoes and onions are golden brown and tender. Turn the potatoes and onions with a spatula several times.

Tzatziki Sauce

MAKES 4 CUPS SAUCE

My neighbor is Greek and shared her family recipe! It has become one of my favorites!

1 pint Greek yogurt

1 cup sour cream

1 hothouse cucumber, peeled, seeded, and finely chopped

3 garlic cloves, minced

2 tablespoons olive oil

1 tablespoon freshly squeezed lemon juice

½ cup chopped fresh mint leaves

Salt and freshly ground black pepper

Mix all the ingredients for the sauce in a medium bowl. Cover and refrigerate for at least one hour.

Chipotle–White Bean Grilled Chicken Chili

SERVES 8

Serve with my yummy cornbread (see page 229). So good!

2 pounds plum tomatoes, quartered

6 tablespoons olive oil

Kosher salt

1 tablespoon minced fresh garlic

2 yellow onions, cut into medium dice

½ red bell pepper, seeds and membranes removed, cut into
    medium dice

½ yellow bell pepper, seeds and membranes removed, cut
    into medium dice

1 serrano chile, seeds and membranes removed, minced

1 pound ground pork

4 grilled chicken breasts, diced

½ chipotle pepper, minced, plus 2 tablespoons
    adobo sauce

1 tablespoon chili powder

1 tablespoon ground cumin

1 teaspoon ground cinnamon

2 teaspoons dried oregano

1 bottle Sierra Nevada Pale Ale

Two 15-ounce cans cannellini beans, drained and rinsed, or
    4 cups cooked dry beans

2 cups chicken stock

2 cups shredded Monterey Jack cheese

1 cup sour cream

1 cup scallions, sliced

1. Preheat the oven to 400°F.

2. Toss the tomatoes with 4 tablespoons of the olive oil and the salt in a bowl. Spray a rimmed baking sheet with non-stick cooking spray. Transfer the tomatoes to the baking sheet and roast for 30 minutes. Remove from the oven and let cool.

3. In a heavy-bottomed pot, heat the remaining 2 table-spoons of olive oil. Add the garlic, onion, peppers, and chile and sauté for 5 minutes. Add the ground pork, breaking it up with a fork, and cook until brown, about 10 minutes. Add the chicken, chipotle, adobo sauce, chili powder, cumin, cinnamon, and oregano and stir to combine. Add the beer, roasted tomatoes, beans, and chicken stock and continue stirring until well combined.

4. Bring the chili to a low boil, reduce the heat, cover, and simmer 1 hour. Season with salt and pepper to taste and continue to cook, uncovered, for 30 minutes. Serve the chili hot, garnished with the cheese, sour cream, and sliced scallions.

*

Buttermilk Cupcakes with
Maple Butter Cream and Bacon

MAKES 12 CUPCAKES

My daughter worked at a fancy cupcake store in Los Angeles last summer and she asked me to create a version of one of her favorites.

Buttermilk Cupcakes

1 ½ cups all-purpose flour

½ teaspoon baking powder

¼ teaspoon baking soda

½ teaspoon salt

8 tablespoons (1 stick) unsalted butter, softened to room
    temperature

½ cup firmly packed brown sugar

¼ cup maple syrup

3 large eggs

¼ cup vegetable oil

1 teaspoon pure vanilla extract

½ cup buttermilk

Maple Butter Cream

8 tablespoons (1 stick) unsalted butter, softened

2 cups confectioners' sugar

1 teaspoon maple extract

1 tablespoon whole milk

6 pieces crisp cooked bacon, crumbled

1. Preheat the oven to 325°F.

2. Line a standard 12-well muffin pan with paper liners. Sift all the dry ingredients together into a bowl. In the bowl of an electric mixer, cream the butter and sugar together on high speed until light and fluffy. Reduce the speed to low, and add the maple syrup and the eggs one at a time. Scrape down the side of the bowl with a spatula and add the vegetable oil and vanilla and continue mixing until combined.

3. Add half of the dry mix, and then half of the buttermilk, and continue mixing on low speed. Then add remaining dry mix and buttermilk. Do not overmix.

4. Divide the batter evenly among the 12 muffin wells. Bake for 20 to 25 minutes, or until a toothpick comes out clean when inserted in the center of a cupcake. Remove from the oven and transfer the cupcakes to a wire rack to cool.

5. In the bowl of an electric mixer, cream the butter until fluffy. Gradually add the sugar, scraping down the sides of the bowl. Add the maple extract and continue mixing. Add a little milk to thin the consistency. Frost each cupcake and garnish with the crumbled bacon.

*

Oatmeal–Dried Cherry Cookies with White Chocolate Chips

MAKES 3 DOZEN COOKIES

I have always loved oatmeal but have never been crazy about raisins. So I substituted dried cherries, and voila!

> 16 tablespoons (2 sticks) unsalted butter, softened to room temperature
> 1 cup granulated sugar
> ½ cup firmly packed light brown sugar
> 2 large eggs
> 2 teaspoons pure vanilla extract
> 1½ cups all-purpose flour
> 1 teaspoon baking soda
> ½ teaspoon salt
> 2½ cups quick or old-fashioned rolled oats
> 1 cup dried cherries
> 1 cup white chocolate chips

1. Preheat the oven to 350°F.

2. In the bowl of an electric mixer, cream the butter with the granulated and brown sugar until fluffy. Add the eggs one at a time and then the vanilla.

3. In a separate bowl sift together the flour, baking soda, and salt. With the mixer on low speed, add the dry ingredients to the bowl with the wet ingredients. Remove the bowl from the mixer and stir in the oats, cherries, and white chocolate chips until incorporated.

2. Using a 1-tablespoon ice cream scoop, or measuring out by the tablespoon, place scoops of the dough onto a cookie sheet, leaving 2 inches between cookies. Bake for 9 to 11 minutes until golden brown. Transfer to a wire rack to cool.

Resources

This section will provide information for all you home chefs to purchase the best possible ingredients, whether you are preparing dinner for one or one hundred!

For Italian cheeses, meats, rice, olive oil, and other specialty items:

EATALY
200 Fifth Avenue
New York, New York 10010
(212) 229-2560
www.eatalyny.com

For spices, bulk and small quantities, and other specialty items:

ROCKY MOUNTAIN SPICE COMPANY
4750 Nome Street, Suite A
Denver, Colorado 80239
(888) 568-4430
www.rockymountainspice.com
www.myspicer.com Online Store

THE SPICE HOUSE
1512 North Wells Street
Chicago, Illinois 60610
(312) 274-0378
www.thespicehouse.com

For fresh fish direct from Hawaii:

HONOLULU FISH COMPANY
824 Gulick Avenue
Honolulu, Hawaii 96819
(808) 833-1123(tel)
(808) 836-1045(fax)
(888) 475-6244(toll-free)
www.honolulufishstore.com

For fresh lobster and other seafood:

HARBOR FISH MARKET
9 Custom House Wharf
Portland, Maine 04101
(800) 370-1790
www.harborfish.com

ASTROLOGY RESOURCES

For those who would like more basic information on astrology, refer to these books that are geared toward the novice astrologer.

The Only Astrology Book You Will Ever Need
  by Joanna Martine Woolfork

*Parkers' Encyclopedia of Astrology: Everything You Ever
  Wanted to Know About Astrology*
  by Derek Parker and Julia Parker

Learning Astrology: An Astrology Book for Beginners
  by Damian Sharp

Index

Açai Berry Smoothie, 8–9

Ahi Tartare on Wonton with Wasabi Crème Fraîche and Tobiko, 87–89

Aioli, 230–232

Alaea Hawaiian Sea Salt, 10

Almond Pound Cake with Caramelized Pears and Mascarpone, 89–91

Apple Crisp à la Mode, 171–172

Apples and Cloves, Roasted Pork Tenderloin with Glazed, 194–195

Aquarius, xxvii, 204–221

Arame Napa Cabbage Slaw with Ginger-Sesame Vinaigrette, 27–28

Aries, xxvii, 1–19

Artichoke Heart Hummus, 12–13

Arugula, and Grana Padano, Pasta Arrabiata with Shrimp, 181–182

Arugula Salad, Shaved Fennel, Blood Orange, and Baby, 71–72

Arugula Salad with Cambozola Cheese, Grilled Cherry and, 133–134

Asian Honey Chicken Kabobs, 158–159

Asparagus with Black Truffle Oil, Grilled, 151–152

astrological guidelines, xxv–xxx

Avocado Dressing, Spicy Shrimp with Hearts of Romaine and Creamy, 35–37

Avocado Salsa, Wild Salmon on Cedar Planks with Corn and, 16–17

Baby Beet Salad over Grilled Portobellos with Brie, Warm, 174–175

Bacon, Buttermilk Cupcakes with Maple Butter Cream and, 238–239

Bacon, Chopped Hearts of Palm with Blue Cheese Dressing and, 219–220

Bacon, Roasted Garlic Mashed Potatoes with Caramelized Onions and, 136–137

Balsamic Syrup, Warm Burrata over Roasted Tomatoes and Basil with Olive Oil and, 130–131

Banana Bread, Madelyn's, 190–191

Basil Salad with Feta Cheese, Cantaloupe, Tomato, and, 54

Basil with Olive Oil and Balsamic Syrup, Warm Burrata over Roasted Tomatoes and, 130–131

beef

Grilled New York Strips with Portobello Mushrooms and Horseradish Sauce, 113–114

Kona Coffee-Rubbed Flank Steak with Cilantro-Lime Vinaigrette, 10–12

Beet Carpaccio and Sherry Vinaigrette, Watercress with, 77–78

Beet Salad over Grilled Portobellos with Brie, Warm Baby, 174–175

Beurre Blanc, 52–53

Bhutanese red rice, 187–188, 203

Biscotti, Chocolate-Dipped Coconut, 176–177

Black Bean Ragout, Creamy Polenta with, 92–94

Black Truffle Oil, Grilled Asparagus with, 151–152

blinis, 152–154

Blood Orange, and Baby Arugula Salad, Shaved Fennel, 71–72

Blueberries and Sour Cream, Cornmeal Pancakes with, 55–56

Blueberry Muffins with Lemon Curd, 212–213

Blue Cheese Dressing and Bacon, Chopped Hearts of Palm with, 219–220

Blue Cheese, Radish, Tomato, and Butterleaf Salad with Bay Shrimp and Maytag, 76–77

Bok Choy with Red Peppers and Oyster Mushrooms, Braised Baby, 110–111

Bordelaise, Lobster, 96–98

Braised Baby Bok Choy with Red Peppers and Oyster Mushrooms, 110–111

Bran Muffins with Pepito Seeds, Pumpkin-, 198–199

Brazil Nuts, Zucchini Bread with Toasted, 28–29

breads

Blueberry Muffins with Lemon Curd, 212–213

Cornmeal Pancakes with Blueberries and Sour Cream, 55–56

Cranberry-Pistachio Scones, 135–136

Madelyn's Banana Bread, 190–191

Pumpkin-Bran Muffins with Pepito Seeds, 198–199

Zesty Chile-Cheese Cornbread, 229–230

Zucchini Bread with Toasted Brazil Nuts, 28–29

Brie, Warm Baby Beet Salad over Grilled Portobellos with, 174–175

Broccolini and Pecorino, Orecchiette Pasta with, 112

Brussels Sprouts, Marinated Roasted, 48–49

Bufala di Mozzarella Napoleon, Heirloom Tomato and, 101–102

Burrata over Roasted Tomatoes and Basil with Olive Oil and Balsamic Syrup, Warm, 130–131

Butterleaf Salad with Bay Shrimp and Maytag Blue Cheese, Radish, Tomato, and, 76–77

Buttermilk Cupcakes with Maple Butter Cream and Bacon, 238–239

Butternut Squash and Wild Rice Pilaf, 39–41

Butternut Squash, Lemon Thyme–Roasted Turkey Breast with, 121–123

Butterscotch Pot de Crème, Celtic Sea Salt, 30–31

Cambozola Cheese, Grilled Cherry and Arugula Salad with, 133–134

Cancer, xxvii, 62–79

Cannellini Bean Ragout with Grilled Rosemary Shrimp, 50–52

Cantaloupe, Tomato, and Basil Salad with Feta Cheese, 54

Caper Relish, Pesto-Crusted Halibut with Tomato, Olive, and, 178–179

Capricorn, xxvii, 183–203

Caramelized Onions and Bacon, Roasted Garlic Mashed Potatoes with, 136–137

Caramelized Pears and Mascarpone, Almond Pound Cake with, 89–91

Carrot Soup, Creamy Coconut-, 214–215

Cauliflower and Maui Onion Gratin with Smoked Gouda, Roasted, 132–133

Caviar Party for Two, 152–154

cedar planks, 16–17

Celtic Sea Salt Butterscotch Pot de Crème, 30–31

Cheese, Lobster Macaroni and, 94–95

Cherry and Arugula Salad with Cambozola Cheese, Grilled, 133–134

Cherry Cookies with White Chocolate Chips, Oatmeal-Dried, 240–241

chicken
Asian Honey Chicken Kabobs, 158–159

Chicken and Napa Cabbage Egg Rolls with Ginger-Chili Vinaigrette, 192–193

Chicken Katsu, 216–218

Chipotle-White Bean Grilled Chicken Chili, 236–237

Grilled Teriyaki Chicken with Pineapple-Mango Salsa, 74–75

Thyme and Panko Crusted Chicken Milanese, 60–61

Chile-Cheese Cornbread, Zesty, 229–230

Chilled Soba Noodle Salad with Tofu and Sesame Vinaigrette, 69–70

Chipotle-White Bean Grilled Chicken Chili, 236–237

Chocolate Chips, Oatmeal-Dried Cherry Cookies with White, 240–241

Chocolate Cocoa Nib Cookies, Double, 9–10

Chocolate-Dipped Coconut Biscotti, 176–177

Chocolate-Rum Pot de Crème, 154–155

Chocolate Shortbread Cookies, Triple Ginger, 157–158

Chopped Hearts of Palm with Blue Cheese Dressing and Bacon, 219–220

Cilantro-Lime Vinaigrette, Kona Coffee-Rubbed Flank Steak with, 10–12

Cinnamon Sauce, 175–176

Cipollini Onions with Cumin, Roasted Potatoes and, 234

Cloves, Roasted Pork Tenderloin with Glazed Apples and, 194–195

Cocktail Nut Mix, Spicy (Cayenne), 215–216

Cocktail Sauce, Coconut- and Macadamia Nut-Crusted Shrimp with Lilikoi, 142–143

Cocoa Nib Cookies, Double Chocolate, 9–10

Coconut- and Macadamia Nut-Crusted Shrimp with Lilikoi Cocktail Sauce, 142–143

Coconut Biscotti, Chocolate-Dipped, 176–177

Coconut-Carrot Soup, Creamy, 214–215

Coconut-Crusted Onaga (Hawaiian Ruby Snapper) with Guava Sauce, 31–33

Coffee-Rubbed Flank Steak with Cilantro-Lime Vinaigrette, Kona, 10–12

Cookies, Double Chocolate Cocoa Nib, 9–10

Cookies, Frosted Lavender and Lemon Zest Shortbread, 116–118

Cookies, Molasses, 196–197

Cookies, Triple Ginger Chocolate Shortbread, 157–158

Cookies with White Chocolate Chips, Oatmeal-Dried Cherry, 240–241

Corn and Avocado Salsa, Wild Salmon on Cedar Planks with, 16–17

Cornbread, Zesty Chile-Cheese, 229–230

Cornmeal Pancakes with Blueberries and Sour Cream, 55–56

Crab Cakes with Julienned Mango and Red Pepper Aioli, 230–232

Crab-Stuffed Opakapaka with Lobster Bordelaise, 96–98

Cranberry-Pistachio Scones, 135–136

Cream Cheese Frosting and Crystallized Ginger, Pumpkin Spice Cupcakes with, 118–119

Creamy Coconut-Carrot Soup, 214–215

Creamy Five Onion Soup, 138–139

Creamy Polenta with Black Bean Ragout, 92–94

Creamy Roasted Red Pepper Sauce with Italian Sausage over Fusilli, 140–141

Crème Brûlée, Matcha, 12–13

Crisp à la Mode, Apple, 171–172

Cucumber-Tomato Salad with Fresh Oregano, 56–57

Cumin, Roasted Potatoes and Cipollini Onions with, 234

desserts

Almond Pound Cake with Caramelized Pears and Mascarpone, 89–91

Apple Crisp à la Mode, 171–172

Buttermilk Cupcakes with Maple Butter Cream and Bacon, 238–239

Celtic Sea Salt Butterscotch Pot de Crème, 30–31

Chocolate-Rum Pot de Crème, 154–155

Matcha Crème Brûlée, 12–13

Panna Cotta with Raspberry Purée, 58–59

Pistachio Mousse Tarts, 220–221

Pumpkin Spice Cupcakes with Cream Cheese Frosting and Crystallized Ginger, 118–119

Strawberry Rose Petal Cupcakes with Rose Butter Cream Frosting, 161–163

Double Chocolate Cocoa Nib Cookies, 9–10

Dried Cherry Cookies with White Chocolate Chips, Oatmeal-, 240–241

Egg Rolls with Ginger-Chili Vinaigrette, Chicken and Napa Cabbage with, 192–193

Fennel, Blood Orange, and Baby Arugula Salad, Shaved, 71–72

Feta Cheese, Cantaloupe, Tomato, and Basil Salad with, 54

Feta Frittata, Spinach and, 200–201

Figs with Gorgonzola, Pancetta-Wrapped, 156

fish and seafood
Ahi Tartare on Wonton with Wasabi Crème Fraîche and Tobiko, 87–89

Coconut-Crusted Onaga (Hawaiian Ruby Snapper) with Guava Sauce, 31–33

Crab-Stuffed Opakapaka with Lobster Bordelaise, 96–98

Grilled Mahi Mahi with Orange and Ginger Beurre Blanc, 52–53

Miso-Marinated Pan-Seared Sea Bass, 211–212

Pesto-Crusted Halibut with Tomato, Olive, and Caper Relish, 178–179

Wild Salmon on Cedar Planks with Corn and Avocado Salsa, 16–17
See also shellfish

Flank Steak with Cilantro-Lime Vinaigrette, Kona Coffee-Rubbed, 10–12

Fontina Frittata, Leek, Potato, Wild Mushroom, and, 72–73

French Green Lentils and Roasted Vegetable Stew, 115–116

Frittata, Leek, Potato, Wild Mushroom, and Fontina, 72–73

Frittata, Spinach and Feta, 200–201

Frosted Lavender and Lemon Zest Shortbread Cookies, 116–118

Garlicky Tofu Stir-Fry, 202–203

Gemini, xxvii, 42–61

Ginger Beurre Blanc, Grilled Mahi Mahi with Orange and, 52–53

Ginger-Chili Vinaigrette, Chicken and Napa Cabbage Egg Rolls with, 192–193

Ginger Chocolate Shortbread Cookies, Triple, 157–158

Ginger Martini for Two, Green Tea, Pineapple, and, 70

Ginger Mignonette Sauce, Malpeque Oysters on the Half Shell with, 159–161

Ginger, Pumpkin Spice Cupcakes with Cream Cheese Frosting and Crystallized, 118–119

Ginger-Sesame Vinaigrette, Arame Napa Cabbage Slaw with, 27–28

Gorgonzola, Pancetta-Wrapped Figs with, 156

Gouda, Roasted Cauliflower and Maui Onion Gratin with Smoked, 132–133

Grana Padano, Pasta Arrabiata
   with Shrimp, Rocket, and,
   181–182
grass-fed beef, 108
Greek yogurt, 235
Green Tea, Pineapple, and Ginger
   Martini for Two, 70
Grilled Asparagus with Black Truffle
   Oil, 151–152
Grilled Cherry and Arugula Salad
   with Cambozola Cheese,
   133–134
Grilled Chicken Chili, Chipotle-
   White Bean, 236–237
Grilled Mahi Mahi with Orange and
   Ginger Beurre Blanc, 52–53
Grilled New York Strips with
   Portobello Mushrooms and
   Horseradish Sauce, 113–114
Grilled Portobellos with Brie,
   Warm Baby Beet Salad over,
   174–175
Grilled Teriyaki Chicken with
   Pineapple-Mango Salsa, 74–75
Guacamole, Lobster, 172–173
Guava Sauce, Coconut-Crusted
   Onaga (Hawaiian Ruby Snapper)
   with, 31–33

Halibut with Tomato, Olive, and
   Caper Relish, Pesto-Crusted,
   178–179
Havarti cheese, 138–139
Hearts of Palm with Blue Cheese
   Dressing and Bacon, Chopped,
   219–220
Herb-Crusted Leg of Lamb,
   232–233
Honey Chicken Kabobs, Asian,
   158–159
Honey Walnut Shrimp, 18–19

Horseradish Sauce, Grilled New York
   Strips with Portobello
   Mushrooms and, 113–114
Hummus, Artichoke Heart, 12–13

ingredient resources, 243–245
Italian Sausage over Fusilli, Creamy
   Roasted Red Pepper Sauce with,
   140–141

Kabobs, Asian Honey Chicken,
   158–159
Kalamata olives, 178–179
Katsu Sauce, 216–218
Kona Coffee-Rubbed Flank Steak
   with Cilantro-Lime Vinaigrette,
   10–12

Lamb, Herb-Crusted Leg of, 232–233
Lamb, Panko Rosemary Crusted Rack
   of, 14–16
Lavender and Lemon Zest Shortbread
   Cookies, Frosted, 116–118
Leek, Potato, Wild Mushroom, and
   Fontina Frittata, 72–73
Lemon Curd, Blueberry Muffins with,
   212–213
Lemon Thyme–Roasted Turkey Breast
   with Butternut Squash, 121–123
Lemon Zest Shortbread Cookies,
   Frosted Lavender and, 116–118
Lentils and Roasted Vegetable Stew,
   French Green, 115–116
Leo, xxvii, 80–102
Libra, xxvii, 124–143
Lilikoi Cocktail Sauce, Coconut- and
   Macadamia Nut-Crusted Shrimp
   with, 142–143
Lime Vinaigrette, Kona Coffee-
   Rubbed Flank Steak with
   Cilantro-, 10–12

Lime, Watermelon with Shaved Maui
Onion and, 79
Lobster Bordelaise, Crab-Stuffed
Opakapaka with, 96–98
Lobster Guacamole, 172–173
Lobster Macaroni and Cheese, 94–95

Macadamia Nut-Crusted Shrimp with
Lilikoi Cocktail Sauce,
Coconut- and, 142–143
Macaroni and Cheese, Lobster,
94–95
Madelyn's Banana Bread, 190–191
Mahi Mahi with Orange and Ginger
Beurre Blanc, Grilled, 52–53
Malpeque Oysters on the Half Shell
with Ginger Mignonette Sauce,
159–161
Mango and Red Pepper Aioli, Crab
Cakes with Julienned, 230–232
Mango Salsa, Grilled Teriyaki
Chicken with Pineapple-, 74–75
Maple Butter Cream and Bacon,
Buttermilk Cupcakes with,
238–239
Marinated Roasted Brussels Sprouts,
48–49
Martini for Two, Green Tea,
Pineapple, and Ginger, 70
Mascarpone, Almond Pound Cake
with Caramelized Pears and,
89–91
Matcha Crème Brûlée, 12–13
Maui Onion and Lime, Watermelon
with Shaved, 79
Maui Onion Gratin with Smoked
Gouda, Roasted Cauliflower and,
132–133
Maytag Blue Cheese, Radish, Tomato,
and Butterleaf Salad with Bay
Shrimp and, 76–77

Meyer Lemon Orzo Risotto, 180–181
Mignonette Sauce, 160
Milanese, Thyme and Panko Crusted
Chicken, 60–61
Molasses Cookies, 196–197
Molokai Sweet Potatoes, Smoked,
218
Mousse Tarts, Pistachio, 220–221
Mozzarella Napoleon, Heirloom
Tomato and Bufala di, 101–102
Muffins with Lemon Curd, Blueberry,
212–213
Muffins with Pepito Seeds, Pumpkin-
Bran, 198–199
Mushroom, and Fontina Frittata,
Leek, Potato, Wild, 72–73
Mushroom Risotto, Wild, 33–35
Mushroom Salad with Pancetta,
Warm Swiss Chard and
Portobello, 38–39
Mushrooms and Horseradish Sauce,
Grilled New York Strips with
Portobello, 113–114
Mushrooms, Braised Baby Bok Choy
with Red Peppers and Oyster,
110–111
Mushrooms with Brie, Warm Baby
Beet Salad over Grilled
Portobello, 174–175

Napa Cabbage Egg Rolls with
Ginger-Chili Vinaigrette,
Chicken and, 192–193
Napa Cabbage Slaw with Ginger-
Sesame Vinaigrette, Arame,
27–28
New York Strips with Portobello
Mushrooms and Horseradish
Sauce, Grilled, 113–114
Nut Mix, Spicy (Cayenne) Cocktail,
215–216

Oatmeal-Dried Cherry Cookies with White Chocolate Chips, 240–241

Okinawan sweet potatoes, 218

Onaga (Hawaiian Ruby Snapper) with Guava Sauce, Coconut-Crusted, 31–33

Onion and Lime, Watermelon with Shaved Maui, 79

Onion Gratin with Smoked Gouda, Roasted Cauliflower and Maui, 132–133

Onions and Bacon, Roasted Garlic Mashed Potatoes with Caramelized, 136–137

Onion Soup, Creamy Five, 138–139

Onions with Cumin, Roasted Potatoes and Cipollini, 234

Opakapaka with Lobster Bordelaise, Crab-Stuffed, 96–98

Orange and Ginger Beurre Blanc, Grilled Mahi Mahi with, 52–53

Orecchiette Pasta with Broccolini and Pecorino, 112

Oregano, Cucumber-Tomato Salad with Fresh, 56–57

Orzo Risotto, Meyer Lemon, 180–181

Oyster Mushrooms, Braised Baby Bok Choy with Red Peppers and, 110–111

Oysters on the Half Shell with Ginger Mignonette Sauce, Malpeque, 159–161

Pancakes with Blueberries and Sour Cream, Cornmeal, 55–56

Pancetta, Warm Swiss Chard and Portobello Salad with, 38–39

Pancetta-Wrapped Figs with Gorgonzola, 156

Panko Rosemary Crusted Rack of Lamb, 14–16

Panna Cotta with Raspberry Purée, 58–59

Pan-Seared Sea Bass, Miso-Marinated, 211–212

Papaya Stuffed with Shrimp Ceviche, 100–101

passion fruit, 142–143

pasta
    Creamy Roasted Red Pepper Sauce with Italian Sausage over Fusilli, 140–141
    Lobster Macaroni and Cheese, 94–95
    Meyer Lemon Orzo Risotto, 180–181
    Orecchiette Pasta with Broccolini and Pecorino, 112
    Pasta Arrabiata with Shrimp, Rocket, and Grana Padano, 181–182

Pears and Mascarpone, Almond Pound Cake with Caramelized, 89–91

Pecorino, Orecchiette Pasta with Broccolini and, 112

Pepito Seeds, Pumpkin-Bran Muffins with, 198–199

Pesto-Crusted Halibut with Tomato, Olive, and Caper Relish, 178–179

Pineapple, and Ginger Martini for Two, Green Tea, 70

Pineapple-Mango Salsa, Grilled Teriyaki Chicken with, 74–75

Pisces, xxvii, 222–241

Pistachio Mousse Tarts, 220–221

Pistachio Scones, Cranberry-, 135–136

Polenta with Black Bean Ragout, Creamy, 92–94

pork
  Chipotle-White Bean Grilled
    Chicken Chili, 236–237
  Roasted Pork Tenderloin with Glazed
    Apples and Cloves, 194–195
  Split Pea Soup with Roasted Pork
    Belly, 120–121
Portobello Mushrooms and
    Horseradish Sauce, Grilled New
    York Strips with, 113–114
Portobello Salad with Pancetta, Warm
    Swiss Chard and, 38–39
Portobellos with Brie, Warm Baby
    Beet Salad over Grilled, 174–175
Potatoes and Cipollini Onions with
    Cumin, Roasted, 234
Potatoes with Caramelized Onions
    and Bacon, Roasted Garlic
    Mashed, 136–137
Pot de Crème, Celtic Sea Salt
    Butterscotch, 30–31
Pot de Crème, Chocolate-Rum,
    154–155
Pound Cake with Caramelized Pears
    and Mascarpone, Almond, 89–91
Pugliese bread, 200–201
Pumpkin-Bran Muffins with Pepito
    Seeds, 198–199
Pumpkin Spice Cupcakes with Cream
    Cheese Frosting and Crystallized
    Ginger, 118–119

Radish, Tomato, and Butterleaf Salad
    with Bay Shrimp and Maytag
    Blue Cheese, 76–77
Ragout, Creamy Polenta with Black
    Bean, 92–94
Ragout with Grilled Rosemary
    Shrimp, Cannellini Bean, 50–52
Raspberry Purée, Panna Cotta with,
    58–59

Red Pepper Aioli, Crab Cakes with
    Julienned Mango and, 230–232
Red Peppers and Oyster Mushrooms,
    Braised Baby Bok Choy with,
    110–111
Red Pepper Sauce with Italian Sausage
    over Fusilli, Creamy Roasted,
    140–141
red rice, Bhutanese, 187–188, 203
Relish, Tomato, Olive, and Caper,
    178–179
Risotto, Meyer Lemon Orzo, 180–181
Risotto, Wild Mushroom, 33–35
roasted dishes
  Creamy Roasted Red Pepper Sauce
    with Italian Sausage over Fusilli,
    140–141
  French Green Lentils and Roasted
    Vegetable Stew, 115–116
  Lemon Thyme–Roasted Turkey
    Breast with Butternut Squash,
    121–123
  Marinated Roasted Brussels
    Sprouts, 48–49
  Roasted Cauliflower and Maui
    Onion Gratin with Smoked
    Gouda, 132–133
  Roasted Garlic Mashed Potatoes
    with Caramelized Onions and
    Bacon, 136–137
  Roasted Pork Tenderloin with
    Glazed Apples and Cloves,
    194–195
  Roasted Potatoes and Cipollini
    Onions with Cumin, 234
  Split Pea Soup with Roasted Pork
    Belly, 120–121
  Warm Burrata over Roasted
    Tomatoes and Basil with Olive
    Oil and Balsamic Syrup,
    130–131

Rocket, and Grana Padano, Pasta
  Arrabiata with Shrimp, 181–182
Rosemary Crusted Rack of Lamb,
  Panko, 14–16
Rosemary Shrimp, Cannellini Bean
  Ragout with Grilled, 50–52
Rose Petal Cupcakes with Rose Butter
  Cream Frosting, Strawberry,
  161–163
Rum Pot de Crème, Chocolate-,
  154–155

Saffron Butter, Seared Scallops with,
  98–99
Sagittarius, xxvii, 164–182
salads
  Arame Napa Cabbage Slaw with
    Ginger-Sesame Vinaigrette,
    27–28
  Cantaloupe, Tomato, and Basil
    Salad with Feta Cheese, 54
  Chilled Soba Noodle Salad with
    Tofu and Sesame Vinaigrette,
    69–70
  Chopped Hearts of Palm with Blue
    Cheese Dressing and Bacon,
    219–220
  Cucumber-Tomato Salad with Fresh
    Oregano, 56–57
  Grilled Cherry and Arugula Salad
    with Cambozola Cheese,
    133–134
  Heirloom Tomato and Bufala di
    Mozzarella Napoleon, 101–102
  Papaya Stuffed with Shrimp
    Ceviche, 100–101
  Radish, Tomato, and Butterleaf
    Salad with Bay Shrimp and
    Maytag Blue Cheese, 76–77
  Shaved Fennel, Blood Orange, and
    Baby Arugula Salad, 71–72

Spicy Shrimp with Hearts of
  Romaine and Creamy Avocado
  Dressing, 35–37
Warm Baby Beet Salad over Grilled
  Portobellos with Brie, 174–175
Warm Burrata over Roasted
  Tomatoes and Basil with Olive
  Oil and Balsamic Syrup,
  130–131
Warm Swiss Chard and Portobello
  Salad with Pancetta, 38–39
Watercress with Beet Carpaccio and
  Sherry Vinaigrette, 77–78
Watermelon with Shaved Maui
  Onion and Lime, 79
Salmon on Cedar Planks with Corn
  and Avocado Salsa, Wild, 16–17
Salsa, Corn and Avocado, 16–17
Salsa, Pineapple-Mango, 74–75
Sauce, Cinnamon, 175–176
Sauce, Tzatziki, 235
Sausage over Fusilli, Creamy Roasted
  Red Pepper Sauce with Italian,
  140–141
Scallops with Saffron Butter, Seared,
  98–99
Scones, Cranberry-Pistachio, 135–136
Scorpio, xxvii, 144–163
Sea Bass, Miso-Marinated Pan-Seared,
  211–212
seafood
  See fish and seafood
Seared Scallops with Saffron Butter,
  98–99
Sesame Vinaigrette, Arame Napa
  Cabbage Slaw with Ginger-, 27–28
Sesame Vinaigrette, Chilled Soba
  Noodle Salad with Tofu and,
  69–70
Shaved Fennel, Blood Orange, and
  Baby Arugula Salad, 71–72

Shaved Maui Onion and Lime,
Watermelon with, 79
shellfish
Cannellini Bean Ragout with
Grilled Rosemary Shrimp, 50–52
Coconut- and Macadamia
Nut-Crusted Shrimp with Lilikoi
Cocktail Sauce, 142–143
Crab Cakes with Julienned Mango
and Red Pepper Aioli, 230–232
Crab-Stuffed Opakapaka with
Lobster Bordelaise, 96–98
Honey Walnut Shrimp, 18–19
Lobster Guacamole, 172–173
Lobster Macaroni and Cheese,
94–95
Malpeque Oysters on the Half Shell
with Ginger Mignonette Sauce,
159–161
Papaya Stuffed with Shrimp
Ceviche, 100–101
Pasta Arrabiata with Shrimp,
Rocket, and Grana Padano,
181–182
Radish, Tomato, and Butterleaf
Salad with Bay Shrimp and
Maytag Blue Cheese, 76–77
Seared Scallops with Saffron Butter,
98–99
Spicy Shrimp with Hearts of
Romaine and Creamy Avocado
Dressing, 35–37
See also fish and seafood
Shortbread Cookies, Frosted Lavender
and Lemon Zest, 116–118
Shortbread Cookies, Triple Ginger
Chocolate, 157–158
shrimp
Cannellini Bean Ragout with
Grilled Rosemary Shrimp,
50–52

Coconut- and Macadamia
Nut-Crusted Shrimp with Lilikoi
Cocktail Sauce, 142–143
Honey Walnut Shrimp, 18–19
Papaya Stuffed with Shrimp
Ceviche, 100–101
Pasta Arrabiata with Shrimp, Rocket,
and Grana Padano, 181–182
Radish, Tomato, and Butterleaf
Salad with Bay Shrimp and
Maytag Blue Cheese, 76–77
Spicy Shrimp with Hearts of
Romaine and Creamy Avocado
Dressing, 35–37
Smoked Gouda, Roasted Cauliflower
and Maui Onion Gratin with,
132–133
Smoked Molokai Sweet Potatoes, 218
Smoothie, Açai Berry, 8–9
Soba Noodle Salad with Tofu and
Sesame Vinaigrette, Chilled,
69–70
Soup, Creamy Coconut-Carrot,
214–215
Soup, Creamy Five Onion, 138–139
Soup with Roasted Pork Belly, Split
Pea, 120–121
Sour Cream, Cornmeal Pancakes with
Blueberries and, 55–56
Spicy (Cayenne) Cocktail Nut Mix,
215–216
Spicy Shrimp with Hearts of Romaine
and Creamy Avocado Dressing,
35–37
Spinach and Feta Frittata, 200–201
Split Pea Soup with Roasted Pork
Belly, 120–121
Stir-Fry, Garlicky Tofu, 202–203
Strawberry Rose Petal Cupcakes with
Rose Butter Cream Frosting,
161–163

Sweet Potatoes, Smoked Molokai, 218

Swiss Chard and Portobello Salad with Pancetta, Warm, 38–39

Tarts, Pistachio Mousse, 220–221

Taurus, xxvii, 20–41

Teriyaki Chicken with Pineapple-Mango Salsa, Grilled, 74–75

Thyme and Panko Crusted Chicken Milanese, 60–61

Thyme–Roasted Turkey Breast with Butternut Squash, Lemon, 121–123

Tobiko, Ahi Tartare on Wonton with Wasabi Crème Fraîche and, 87–89

Tofu and Sesame Vinaigrette, Chilled Soba Noodle Salad with, 69–70

Tofu Stir-Fry, Garlicky, 202–203

Tomato, and Basil Salad with Feta Cheese, Cantaloupe, 54

Tomato and Bufala di Mozzarella Napoleon, Heirloom, 101–102

Tomato, and Butterleaf Salad with Bay Shrimp and Maytag Blue Cheese, Radish, 76–77

Tomatoes and Basil with Olive Oil and Balsamic Syrup, Warm Burrata over Roasted, 130–131

Tomato, Olive, and Caper Relish, Pesto-Crusted Halibut with, 178–179

Tomato Salad with Fresh Oregano, Cucumber-, 56–57

Triple Ginger Chocolate Shortbread Cookies, 157–158

Turkey Breast with Butternut Squash, Lemon Thyme–Roasted, 121–123

Tzatziki Sauce, 235

Vegetable Stew, French Green Lentils and Roasted, 115–116

Virgo, xxvii, 103–123

Walnut Shrimp, Honey, 18–19

Warm Baby Beet Salad over Grilled Portobellos with Brie, 174–175

Warm Burrata over Roasted Tomatoes and Basil with Olive Oil and Balsamic Syrup, 130–131

Warm Swiss Chard and Portobello Salad with Pancetta, 38–39

Wasabi Crème Fraîche and Tobiko, Ahi Tartare on Wonton with, 87–89

Watercress with Beet Carpaccio and Sherry Vinaigrette, 77–78

Watermelon with Shaved Maui Onion and Lime, 79

White Bean Grilled Chicken Chili, Chipotle-, 236–237

Wild Mushroom, and Fontina Frittata, Leek, Potato, 72–73

Wild Mushroom Risotto, 33–35

Wild Rice Pilaf, Butternut Squash and, 39–41

Wild Salmon on Cedar Planks with Corn and Avocado Salsa, 16–17

Wonton with Wasabi Crème Fraîche and Tobiko, Ahi Tartare on, 87–89

yogurt, 8–9, 235

Zesty Chile-Cheese Cornbread, 229–230

Zucchini Bread with Toasted Brazil Nuts, 28–29